Provision Mapping

This highly practical book contains all the guidance and resources a school will need in order to implement an efficient and effective system of pupil progress tracking and evaluative Provision Mapping. It is a tried and tested system that has been shown to improve outcomes for all pupils, including those with special educational needs (SEN), and sits at the very heart of school self-evaluation.

Throughout this book, teachers will find achievable solutions to the problems schools face in trying to ensure that their practice results in all pupils making good progress. Anne Massey has adapted the original version of Provision Mapping and developed it into a more evaluative framework that links a number of school improvement actions together. All the recommendations in this book have been tried and tested in primary schools, and have been proven to:

- bring about better progress and engagement for all pupils;
- provide an enhanced understanding of inclusion by teachers;
- improve communication between the school, parents and the Local Authority;
- reduce bureaucracy and paperwork for SENCOs;
- foster an improved understanding of 'value for money'.

Headteachers, senior managers, leadership teams, SENCOs and other educational professionals will find the guidance and support provided by this toolkit invaluable. *Provision Mapping* will also be of value to those studying the more SEN-specific postgraduate diplomas or Masters level qualifications.

Anne Massey, an experienced SENCO and school leader, is currently employed as a Local Authority School Improvement Adviser with a focus on inclusion in Kent, UK. She has spoken at national conferences and delivers training on Provision Mapping.

National Association for Special Educational Needs (nasen)

nasen is a professional membership association that supports all those who work with or care for children and young people with special and additional educational needs. Members include teachers, teaching assistants, support workers, other educationalists, students and parents.

nasen supports its members through policy documents, journals, its magazine *Special!*, publications, professional development courses, regional networks and newsletters. Its website contains more current information such as responses to government consultations. **nasen**'s published documents are held in very high regard both in the UK and internationally.

Other titles published in association with the National Association for Special Educational Needs (nasen):

Brilliant Ideas for Using ICT in the Inclusive Classroom
Sally McKeown and Angela McGlashon
2011/pb: 978-0-415-67254-2

Language for Learning in the Secondary School
A practical guide for supporting students with speech, language and communication needs
Sue Hayden and Emma Jordan
2012/pb: 978-0-415-61975-2

ADHD
All your questions answered: A complete handbook for SENCOs and teachers
Fintan O'Regan
2012/pb: 978-0-415-59770-8

Assessing Children with Specific Learning Difficulties
A teacher's practical guide
Gavin Reid, Gad Elbeheri and John Everatt
2012/pb: 978-0-415-67027-2

Using Playful Practice to Communicate with Special Children
Margaret Corke
2012/pb: 978-0-415-68767-6

The Equality Act for Educational Professionals
A simple guide to disability and inclusion in schools
Geraldine Hills
2012/pb: 978-0-415-68768-3

More Trouble with Maths
A teacher's complete guide to identifying and diagnosing mathematical difficulties
Steve Chinn
2012/pb: 978-0-415-67013-5

Dyslexia and Inclusion
Classroom approaches for assessment, teaching and learning, second editon
Gavin Reid
2012/pb: 978-0-415-60758-2

Provision Mapping

Improving outcomes in primary schools

Anne Massey

 Routledge
Taylor & Francis Group

LONDON AND NEW YORK

 nasen
Helping Everyone Achieve

First published 2013
by Routledge
2 Park Square, Milton Park, Abingdon, Oxon OX14 4RN

Simultaneously published in the USA and Canada
by Routledge
711 Third Avenue, New York, NY 10017

Routledge is an imprint of the Taylor & Francis Group, an informa business

British Library Cataloguing in Publication Data
A catalogue record for this book is available from the British Library

Library of Congress Cataloging in Publication Data
Massey, Anne.
  Provision mapping : improving outcomes in primary schools / Anne Massey.
       p. cm. — (David fulton / nasen)
    Includes index.
  1. Educational evaluation—Great Britain. 2. School improvement programs—
Great Britain. I. Title.
  LB2822.75.M383 2013
  379.1′580941—dc23   2012022399

ISBN: 978-0-415-53028-6 (hbk)
ISBN: 978-0-415-53030-9 (pbk)
ISBN: 978-0-203-07875-4 (ebk)

Typeset in Bembo
by Keystroke, Station Road, Codsall, Wolverhampton

Contents

Preface

Why does your school need this book?

- Do you have systems for tracking pupil progress embedded in your school?
- Do you know what progress is being made by individuals and by groups in your school?
- Are you doing something about progress that has stalled or is inadequate?
- Do all class teachers have full responsibility and accountability for all pupils in their class, including those with SEN?
- Can you tell what the impact is of your additional interventions?
- Do you know whether you are getting value for money?
- Are your governors sufficiently well informed to be able to make suitable challenge?
- Are parents confident that your school is doing all it can to meet their children's needs?

If not, then this book is for you.

The system of evaluative Provision Mapping described in this book works – it helps schools to make the best provision for their most vulnerable pupils and ensures that all pupils, irrespective of their ability, are set challenging targets and make good progress. It leads to:

- greater responsibility of class teachers for the progress of all pupils in their class;
- greater involvement of class teachers in making provision for pupils with SEN;
- reduced bureaucracy and workload for SENCOs;
- enhanced school self-evaluation and development planning;
- improved communication with parents, governors, Ofsted and the LA.

These are brave claims, but Provision Mapping really does work. It is principally a system that can be personalised to meet the needs of your school, but it will lead to improved outcomes in any primary school irrespective of its size, location or Ofsted category.

Acknowledgements

With grateful thanks to all the headteachers and SENCOs in schools throughout Kent who have been instrumental in the further development and refinement of this system of Provision Mapping; in particular to Marden Primary School and Ridge View Special School.

To Alwen Coventry, for the way she inspired me and countless others, and for leading me down this path; to Diana Robinson, for her awesome knowledge, skill and her unshakeable faith in me, and to Peter Grimes, whose practical support and encouragement made such a difference.

Special thanks to my patient and constant friends, in particular Mary Murphy and Carol Fullwood.

This book is dedicated to the memory of my parents and to the next generation: my beautiful daughters Rachel, Rebecca and Beth, whose love and laughter kept me going.

Chapter 1

Introduction to evaluative Provision Mapping

Provision Mapping is not new. The original version of a Provision Map, and one with which many schools may be familiar, was proposed by Gross and White in 2003 in their book *Special Educational Needs and School Improvement*. They showed how a school could list the provision it made and demonstrate the cost in time and money of each intervention. Over the intervening years many schools and even some local authorities have created their own Provision Maps but in most cases it would appear that the full potential of a Provision Map, as a tool to support school self-evaluation and strategic management, has not been realised.

My own experience of Provision Mapping began in a primary school where I was both SENCO and part of the leadership team. When Provision Mapping was first proposed by my local authority I experienced frustration with what appeared to be yet another pointless paper exercise; I was already writing 64 IEPs (Individual Education Plan) and I was now being asked to provide a costed Provision Map. I was very concerned that the IEPs seemed largely irrelevant as no one, least of all the pupils, could ever remember the targets; the Provision Map seemed to be nothing more than a list of interventions with a costing exercise that was time-consuming, difficult and potentially damaging as my school tried to use it to justify its SEN spending. The true evidence about whether or not the additional provision being made was having an impact was not known, since the assessment of pupil progress that was carried out was not linked to the outcome of interventions.

The Provision Mapping system I present in this book has emerged from efforts to link an adaptation of the original concept of a Provision Map to the principles of school improvement. It could be considered to be the 'Weight Watchers' of education, an analogy that demonstrates how and why this system will work so well. The principles are the same as those of the Weight Watchers programme which has been proven to be more effective than any other regime in bringing about weight loss (*The Lancet* 2011, pp. 1485–1492).

- Initial weighing (assessment) reveals whether there is a problem that needs addressing (intervention).
- Only through regular weighing (assessment) on accurate scales can you identify whether weight loss (progress) is being achieved.
- By analysing what you are doing (data analysis) with others (pupil progress review meetings) you can determine whether you need to change your diet and/or exercise (classroom teaching and/or intervention) to improve weight loss (progress).
- Effectiveness is enhanced if any problems with dieting are discussed within a group (professional development meetings) in a structured and collaborative way.

- You need to repeatedly weigh yourself (assessment) and analyse your progress (pupil progress review) over intervals of equal length to see whether what you have done has worked and to ensure that progress is sustained.
- Once you have reached your target weight (on track for end-of-year target) you will be able to cease the diet (intervention) and maintain your correct weight through sensible eating and an exercise regime (good classroom teaching).
- All your efforts will be improved by sharing your aims and outcome with others (parents, governors, etc.).

Over the past 20 years or so there has been a steady stream of new programmes, strategies or initiatives imposed upon schools by successive governments with little regard for schools' individual characteristics, needs or differences. This has led undoubtedly to 'initiative overload' and has given rise to an understandably weary scepticism among many school staff; so much so that many have come to treat any new proposal with, at best extreme caution and a sense of déjà vu, and at worst negativity or hostility. This Provision Mapping system is different: in fact, wherever it has been introduced to schools it has almost always been received with an uncharacteristic enthusiasm, even by the most resistant of teaching staff, and, once adopted, teachers have commented that it 'makes sense' and 'puts them back in control'.

Many of the elements of the system described in this book will be familiar, since many originate from the Improving Schools Programme (ISP) (DfES 2004). You may, indeed should, already have some of them embedded in your school. Although the product of a previous government's agenda, the aspects of the ISP programme that have been incorporated into this system (tracking progress, whole school CPD, focus on teaching and learning, and planned arrangements for monitoring, evaluation and review of pupil progress) are those that are fundamental to ensuring that all pupils will attain well and will endure, irrespective of government agenda.

If you already have many of the elements of this system embedded in your school why do you need this book? Although many schools have encountered some or most of the elements of the system before, it appears that few have realised the potential of linking the different aspects together into something that will be as consistently effective in driving school improvement as this system is.

My emerging view of the need for a strategic, self-evaluative, collaborative approach to managing intervention was influenced by Ekins and Grimes, who had taken Gross and White's ideas further and identified the need to facilitate a simple and achievable process for monitoring, challenging and improving pupil progress. They stressed the importance of linking systems together to bring about school improvement and noted that when conducted in isolation 'the value that the systems hold for enabling innovative, meaningful and strategic whole-school development can be lost' (Ekins and Grimes 2009, p. 2). In the following chapters you will find some of the rationale and theoretical links that endorse this system as a method of improving outcomes, but principally I intend to provide the guidance and resources necessary to enable headteachers, SENCOs, senior leaders and teachers to implement it in a sustainable and easy way, so that it can sit at the heart of school self-evaluation and support future development

Raising standards

It has long been argued that there are tensions between the policy drive to raise standards and strategies to ensure that all children are fully participating and achieving in all aspects of life in mainstream schools (Ainscow *et al.* 2006). However, the reality for schools is that they need to operate within a context driven by a standards agenda. I do not propose to explore this controversy in great depth here but wish to acknowledge that, although it may appear at odds with inclusion, this system is underpinned by the principle that 'tracking leads to success' (DfES 2007) which, I will demonstrate, can and does enhance inclusion.

Data collection and analysis is essential to understanding how to bring about improvements in pupil progress. Recent research has shown that 'inclusion can be entirely compatible with high levels of achievement and, furthermore, that combining the two is not only possible but essential if all children are to have the opportunity to participate fully in education' (Black-Hawkins *et al.* 2007). In 2011 the government clearly stated its aims for all pupils with SEN and disability in its Green Paper, *Support and Aspiration: A New Approach to Special Educational Needs and Disability* (DfE 2011b). This was influenced by the findings of the Ofsted review of SEN 2010, *A Statement is Not Enough* (Ofsted 2010c), and the same principles are a strong feature of the current Ofsted evaluation schedule. The subsidiary guidance to inspectors and an analysis of early inspection outcomes under the 2012 inspection framework indicate strongly that in order to be considered good, schools will need to not only track the performance of any vulnerable groups but narrow the gap between the outcomes of those groups and all pupils within the school, and that the school's vulnerable groups should be making better progress than similar groups nationally. However, achieving such aims is not easy, and 'doing so can make great demands on those who work in classrooms and schools' (Black-Hawkins *et al.* 2007). I am confident that a school that fully embeds this Provision Mapping system will develop greater capacity for narrowing the outcomes gap in a time-saving, coherent and effective way.

The government has indicated a commitment to reducing bureaucracy, and Provision Mapping can certainly help to achieve this if used properly. This method of Provision Mapping ensures that it is not the additional bureaucratic burden schools originally thought it to be (a belief still held by many SENCOs); it is, instead, something that will support schools in making links between a number of processes, to collate information, reduce paperwork and ensure that meetings are focused and effective.

Although the enticement of reduced bureaucracy may be what prompts many schools to implement this system, I have found that its greatest value is its ability to stimulate and bring about change. It is my experience that most schools have at least one teacher who struggles to understand the needs of pupils with SEN and/or those who are underachieving in their class, and does not differentiate appropriately or make adequate provision for them. Historically, many teachers have been happy to abdicate responsibility for such pupils to the SENCO or to learning support staff and perversely, in schools where the SENCO is particularly strong, this has tended to happen even more frequently.

While good leaders will be able to motivate and inspire the majority of their staff, these 'hard to shift' teachers are often the most difficult to engage in any dialogue of self-improvement and remain entrenched in a pattern of teaching that does not meet the needs of all pupils. This system has been proven to create the right conditions for such change and brings a structure and timetable that, if adhered to, ensures that change *will* take place.

The government's Green Paper proposes changes to SEN classification and removing School Action and School Action Plus in favour of a single category of SEN. Many SENCOs fear that this will lead to a reduction in support for some SEN pupils. While the impact of such a change remains to be seen, I believe that if schools use this system of Provision Mapping they will ensure that everyone, irrespective of SEN, will be supported and the need for any classification of SEN could disappear altogether. In her book *Beating Bureaucracy in Special Educational Needs* (2008), Jean Gross cited an example of how a secondary school had removed Statements yet retained and even enhanced the provision made for the most vulnerable pupils. In their 2010 SEN review, Ofsted stressed that the effect of SEN labelling is often to lower aspiration both by and of the pupil and stated that the inconsistency in the identification of SEN does not matter if 'the total package of services and support is appropriately customised to each pupil's individual needs' (Ofsted 2010). Through the use of this system the school will focus on the needs of *all* pupils, making no distinction between SEN and non-SEN other than to ensure that the statutory duties are complied with for all pupils with a Statement. If the government's proposals to implement Education, Health and Care plans for pupils come to fruition, Provision Mapping will provide an excellent vehicle for the evaluation of the impact of education services and could be adapted to include the services provided by other agencies.

This is therefore a system for all – not just SEN – that should address problems early and as they arise and not once they are well entrenched. It should put SEN firmly back into the classroom. It will mean that all teachers will feel more in control of what happens to pupils in their class – the pupils shouldn't disappear out to interventions that the teacher has no part in planning or evaluating.

If this system is fully adopted it will lead to:

- improved class teaching;
- teachers being responsible for the outcomes of all pupils in their class – not passing SEN to anyone else;
- identification of gaps in expertise within the school and improved understanding of training needs;
- better understanding of what pupils feel works for them;
- smarter target setting;
- better self-evaluation and planning for improvement;
- better understanding of whether the school is getting value for money;
- better information for parents, governors, Ofsted and the LA;
- improved ability to reallocate resources to points of greatest need.

It should reduce:

- removal from class for intervention;
- in-class 'velcro TA' support (a TA sitting next to a child in all lessons, following them through unstructured times and communicating with others on their behalf);
- work for SENCOs;
- initiatives that seem unrelated to other school processes.

This system of evaluative Provision Mapping is a year-long process with six separate elements, all of which will be covered one by one over the next six chapters. The final chapter will explain all the links to other school processes and how best to implement the system in your school.

Chapter 2

Assessment

The key to the success of Provision Mapping is assessment that is robust and reliable. The current established and familiar measures of attainment – A levels, GCSEs, National Curriculum levels and sub-levels and P-levels – have long provided schools with standardised assessment bench-marks. Even though there is a strong indication from the current government that these may be replaced by alternative systems for accreditation and radically different measures of attainment in the future, the need to understand the progress being made towards expected outcomes will continue to be necessary and will need to rely on accurate assessment. This book will focus on the use of National Curriculum levels and sub-levels as, at the time of writing, it is the current measure of achievement. However, this system of Provision Mapping could be adapted to use any standardised measure of progress and attainment.

Hopefully all schools now carry out in-class assessment several times a year and use these data to measure progress, so this chapter is not aimed at explaining why you must assess; instead it will encourage you to consider the reliability of your current assessment as an indicator of pupil progress.

Pupil progress tracking will not be of any use if the data generated are insecure. To return to the Weight Watchers analogy, if you were attempting to lose weight and you found that your scales were unreliable or inaccurate you would quickly adjust them or get new ones – you would want to know to the ounce or gram exactly how much weight loss had been achieved through all that abstinence and self-denial! Assessment is the scales of education – measuring accurately how much progress has been made relies on scales that are used at frequent and equal intervals and regularly calibrated or moderated to guarantee their accuracy. This chapter will focus on how to ensure that your assessment is reliable and manageable, and how to be confident that it is telling you what you need to know.

One of the ways that this system of Provision Mapping is intended to reduce workload and bureaucracy is by measuring two aspects of progress simultaneously – progress in class and progress made by pupils in interventions. Intervention that has been effective will have succeeded in re-engaging the pupil with learning, brought them back on track and had an impact on progress in NC levels. This system is designed to make use of the assessment of reading, writing and numeracy, carried out in class several times a year to also evaluate the impact of interventions. There are, however, a few interventions, such as those aimed at addressing social, emotional and behavioural difficulties, physical development or speech and language needs, that will require additional testing to establish whether sufficient impact has been achieved. These methods will be outlined later in this chapter. Throughout this book I will refer to the school year as divided into six terms as per the Kent model, where each long, traditional term has been divided into two shorter terms numbered one to six.

Questions that will be answered in this chapter

- Which method should be used for assessment?
- How can we ensure that our assessment is reliable enough?
- When should we assess?
- What should we assess?
- Do we need any other forms of assessment?

Which method should be used for assessment?

Whatever measure is used to gauge attainment there are principally two different methods of assessment available: testing and teacher assessment.

A large number of schools still rely on the test method. Some tend to use past SATs papers, while others have bought into one of the many different commercially available tests, most of which bear a resemblance to SATs tests. Schools that use tests say they provide a sense of reliability; the tests are standardised and provide an externally validated tool with which to measure attainment. But if a school is going to use tests to assess pupil performance are they reliable enough?

In its aim to raise standards in primary and secondary schools the government currently relies on the analysis of statutory assessment (test) data to generate the measures of success (standards) against which it holds schools to account. The stakes are high: if a school falls below the expected standards it could ultimately be subject to an Academy Order or face threat of closure. Ofsted, too, relies heavily on the standardised national test data when judging the quality of a school. In its 2012 framework this reliance is such that, for schools which have been previously judged by Ofsted to be good or better, a summary judgement of a school's performance between inspections will be largely based on an analysis of attainment and progress data generated from the nationally standardised tests and presented in the school's RAISEOnline (Ofsted 2012).

If a single measurement of attainment is to be relied upon so heavily we must be certain that the results given are reliable and valid. We therefore need to ask a number of critical questions: do tests measure accurately, do they measure the right things and does their use improve outcomes? If not, is it appropriate for schools to choose to use tests as an assessment method to evaluate attainment and progress between Key Stages?

The sudden scrapping of the Key Stage 3 tests in 2008 and the more recent alterations to the KS2 tests were, in some part, in response to revelations of inaccuracy and unreliability. The accuracy of National SATs testing has consistently been called into question since their inception. For example, research in 2000 showed that almost 30 per cent of test results were inaccurate (Black *et al.* 2008).

But it is not just risk of inaccuracy that should cause schools to hesitate to use tests; there are other reasons why the use of SATs papers or tests would be an unsuitable method for measurement of in-year attainment and progress:

- Past or non-statutory SATs papers, administered earlier in the year than Term 5 or 6, will not give an accurate assessment of pupil knowledge, as the full curriculum will not have been covered.
- Standardised tests cannot generally be administered as frequently over the course of the year as is necessary in order for the school to keep a close eye on progress.
- Commercial testing packages, if administered as discrete tests and not as part of a programme of learning, could have been constructed to test aspects that the pupil has not been taught.
- Testing can be time expensive.
- Pupil anxiety over testing can lead to inaccurate outcomes.
- Testing does not measure learning but only measures a particular window of learning; much of what is learned by the child in certain subjects is difficult to measure in tests and so is left out.

The alternative to testing is teacher assessment which Black *et al.* indicated was the most appropriate and reliable way of measuring attainment. They stated:

> [T]eachers can sample the range of a pupil's work more fully than can any assessment instruments devised by an agency external to the school. This enhances both reliability (because it provides more evidence than is available through externally-devised assessment instruments) and validity (it provides a wider range of evidence). Together maximum validity and optimal reliability contribute to the dependability of assessments – the confidence that can be placed in them.
>
> (www.tlrp.org/pub/documents/assessment.pdf)

Although I agree with Black *et al.* and generally advise schools to use teacher assessment for the purposes of this system, as with testing, it is not always as reliable as it should be and the school selecting this as a method of assessment should still exercise caution. In 2009 the QCA published research based on the 2006 and 2007 English writing tasks that analysed the number of times markers disagreed on the student's level, revealing that almost half of the English writing papers could have been misclassified (Qualifications and Curriculum Authority 2009). If there is this level of disagreement between accredited markers then schools should question the reliability of their own levelling and keep it under constant review.

The introduction of tools for teacher assessment, APP (assessing pupil progress), by the QCA in 2004 has gone a long way towards transforming the willingness of schools to relinquish testing and has led many to adopt teacher assessment as their chosen method of in-year and in-Key Stage assessment. Prior to the introduction of APP, teacher assessment was often considered too 'hit and miss' to be relied upon for the levelling of pupil attainment. However, the prescribed nature and focus on moderation built into APP has contributed to schools' growing confidence in the use of teacher assessment to ascribe levels accurately. The constant assessment aspect has led to much greater opportunities to measure progress more frequently and to identify gaps in learning more accurately.

Assessment for learning (AfL)has been endorsed by the present government; 'skilled and precise assessment of pupils' work – both of the level at which children are working and of what they should be learning next – is an essential part of good teaching' (DfE 2010). The in-year assessments carried out by schools need to be part of ongoing assessments for learning; they should be formative as well as summative and should be used not just to measure attainment but to inform planning and determine further action. In 1999, the Assessment Reform Group defined assessment for learning as:

> [T]he process of seeking and interpreting evidence for use by learners and their teachers to decide where the learners are in their learning, where they need to go and how best to get there.
>
> (Assessment Reform Group 1999)

A strong system of teacher assessment such as APP will fulfil these criteria by providing both a snapshot assessment of where pupils are in their learning at a given point in time (the assessment information used in pupil progress tracking) and also what they would need to do to improve (the assessment information used to set targets for interventions).

Many schools would argue that early exposure to testing prepares children for the many tests and examinations they will encounter as they progress through the school system. While I acknowledge that familiarisation with testing is important, because testing is unreliable, cannot be carried out regularly enough, narrows aspects of learning and is time expensive I remain unconvinced that schools should select testing over teacher assessment. However, there are many schools that use both methods of assessment, either alternating them or using them simultaneously. While using and comparing both methods simultaneously gives strong data and enables schools to identify bias or error (high or low levelling) in tests, it is time-consuming and still potentially open to inaccuracy, since the frequency with which testing can be conducted is usually limited. If tests are alternated with teacher assessment it would be like weighing oneself on a different set of scales each time; you can only really assess progress if you use the same measure or scales consistently.

How can we be sure our assessment is reliable enough?

This is the million-dollar question. Even though your school may have well-established methods of assessment every school leadership team should consider this question regularly because if the data are not reliable, measurement of progress cannot be reliable.

For schools using tests to assess attainment they should consider the issues raised earlier, namely:

- Can we use it often enough?
- Does it test what has been taught?
- Will it give us the information necessary to plan for future learning?
- Have we taken steps to eliminate marker error?
- Can we detect any error in levelling? For instance, does this test give a level significantly lower or higher than that achieved by the same pupils sitting a different test or via teacher assessment?
- Is everyone using the same test?

I believe teacher assessment to be the most appropriate method of assessment for the purposes of this system and will focus on that method for the remainder of this book. Even though teacher assessment is generally more reliable, there are still a number of issues for schools to consider:

- Do we moderate teacher assessment often enough and well enough?
- Does everyone know what each level 'looks like' in reading, writing and numeracy?
- Do we moderate with a wide enough range of partners?
- Do the tasks we use to assess learning measure the right aspects of learning?
- Do we make summative assessments often enough and at regular intervals?
- Do all teachers use the same methods for teacher assessment and do they all apply the same criteria?

How then can schools ensure reliability in teacher assessment? There is no magic formula; there simply needs to be thorough knowledge of the level descriptors coupled with regular moderation. Although moderation is key to ensuring assessment is reliable it is often something that schools overlook or sideline, prioritising other activities instead. This is a mistake. Moderation should be a very high priority for all schools and should be time-tabled into the school's calendar at the start of the year. The Department for Education states:

> Moderation helps teachers to be confident that they are applying accurate and consistent standards when making their teacher assessment judgments. It also helps to ensure the teacher assessment results are fair for pupils and useful for schools and others who evaluate performance and progress.
>
> (DfE 2012, accessed 9 April 2012)

One way of ensuring that all curriculum subjects are moderated regularly enough could be to prepare a moderation timetable (Table 2.1). Moderation events should be planned once per term: moderation of reading, writing and numeracy to take place in alternate terms with moderation of three other subjects (for example, science, geography, speaking and listening) taking place in the remaining terms according to a two- or three-year cycle.

The moderation activities for reading, writing and maths should involve all teachers and as many learning support staff as possible, particularly those who deliver literacy and numeracy interventions. They will need to be fully aware of what each literacy and numeracy level 'looks like' if they are to support pupils in achieving those levels. One simple but effective way of ensuring that staff and pupils know what each level 'looks like' is to create a display around the school of anonymised pieces of work annotated to show the specific criteria linked to each level. This acts as a reference tool for pupils and staff

Table 2.1 Three-year moderation timetable (primary)

Year	Term 1	Term 2	Term 3	Term 4	Term 5	Term 6
1	Reading	Speaking and listening	Writing	Science	Maths	History
2	Geography	Reading	RE	Writing	PE	Maths
3	Maths	ICT	Reading	Art	Writing	Music

alike and ensures that all are aware of what they are aiming for when aspiring to achieve the next level in writing or numeracy.

Moderation *in* school is essential but so too is moderation *with* other schools. In particular, moderation of pupils who are working below NC levels on P scales needs to take place in a wider forum, as most mainstream primary schools will have too few examples of work at that level to enable them to make comparisons. Ofsted makes clear in its guidance to inspectors that this level of inter-school moderation is to be expected when it instructs them to:

> find out about the rigour of the moderation procedures for any teacher assessment including P-scales (at minimum this should be across the school, best practice is across local authority/region/or group of schools).
>
> (Ofsted 2010a)

The other merits of inter-school moderation are that it creates opportunities for infant and junior, primary and secondary schools to moderate together which should enable them to build confidence in each other's judgements and create an atmosphere of trust in the levels that are ascribed to children on transfer. The most recent guidance from Ofsted indicates that junior schools should be baselining pupils on entry to accurately gauge starting-points and demonstrate progress over time.

> Key Stage 1 assessment results are the most important source of evidence on prior attainment. However, inspectors should take account of any assessments the school makes of pupils' attainment on entry and check that the school has quickly and correctly identified those pupils that did not meet the Key Stage 1 thresholds and, conversely, those that exceeded the thresholds.
>
> (Ofsted Subsidiary Guidance 2012)

This guidance could be interpreted by junior schools in such a way that they retest all pupils on entry but I do not believe this will be necessary if collaborative moderation over time between schools has taken place. However, there may well be some pupils whose low or high levels give cause for further testing/assessment on entry.

Selecting the right tasks to use for teacher assessment is vital. One of the problems often cited with the use of tests to assess maths is that the test does not cover the aspect of numeracy most recently taught and therefore cannot truly measure progress. However, similar problems can arise in using teacher assessment: if each area of learning such as 'shape, space and measure' or 'calculation' is assessed separately over the course of a year, how can progress be tracked from one area to a different area? APP can support schools in this by enabling teachers to ascribe a level based on their knowledge of the levels and their evidence from moderation.

When to assess?

When to assess is really two questions: with what frequency should assessment take place and when in the year should assessments be carried out? The frequency with which assessment should take place is often debated. Those schools in Ofsted category or falling below the government's standards are generally expected to assess pupil progress six times a year. Ekins and Grimes believe that three times per year is effective and recommend this pattern; one that allows sufficient time for learning to occur before progress is measured (2009, p. 47). But the timing of the assessments can also have an impact on the frequency. As previously mentioned, Ofsted expects schools to track progress from starting points over time and implies in its supplementary guidance for inspectors that early baseline assessment should take place, particularly for pupils on entry to junior schools. Many schools that have confidence in the ability of the feeder schools to level pupils accurately would be content to use prior attainment data as the baseline and make the first assessment at the end of Term 1, repeated again at the end of each term: a total of six assessments. Ofsted's expectation that junior schools will baseline on entry would indicate that an early assessment should be carried out – at the start of Term 1. If the school were then to carry out further assessments at the end of each term that would mean a total of seven assessments for that year. This would seem somewhat excessive but, if the prior attainment data were thought to be unreliable and no initial baseline was carried out, opportunities to provide support in the early weeks would have been lost.

The timing of assessment is worth schools considering at length. I believe that the optimum time for a first assessment is towards the end of Term 1. This is obviously the case for any school that intends to assess six times per year but for those that intend to assess less frequently (three or four times) the first assessment will still need to be early on in the year so that any fall-back from the previous year may be swiftly identified and addressed.

Therefore, for each pattern of assessment the first measurement should be towards the end of Term 1 and subsequent assessments must take place at regular intervals so that the interval over which progress is measured is broadly equal. I recommend to schools that intend carrying out assessments three times per year that they take place at the end of Term 1, half-way through Term 3 and then Term 5 (which will be aligned with SATs). However, this would mean that the pupils' end of year assessment was made prematurely, so generally I recommend a minimum of four assessments – following the pattern described above with an additional assessment made at the end of term 6 and used to inform planning for the following year.

An example of a simplistic assessment calendar is given in Table 2.2.

Table 2.2 Assessment calendar

Model	Term 1	Term 2	Term 3	Term 4	Term 5	Term 6
Six times per year	assess	assess	assess	assess	assess	assess
Three times per year	assess		assess		assess	
Four times per year	assess		assess		assess	assess

However, as term lengths vary somewhat, the main consideration should be to ensure that intervals are broadly equal and that the timing of the assessment is aligned to fit in with other related activities – for instance, parent consultation should follow soon after an assessment so that parents are being given the most up-to-date progress and attainment information. Further details on how to timetable the assessments will be discussed in later chapters and example timetables are found in Chapter 8.

What to assess?

Class-based assessments, either test or teacher assessment, are usually focused on measuring attainment in reading, writing and maths. Some schools also assess speaking and listening, particularly in Key Stage 1, and some assess science. For the purposes of discussing pupils whose progress has stalled or who are making inadequate progress, we usually refer to progress in reading, writing and maths and therefore the class-based assessments will be sufficient for the purpose. If, as I propose, schools use these assessments to measure the impact of interventions as well, they will certainly be able to measure the impact of the interventions on those areas of learning but not on the wider aspects of development. As I stressed earlier, an aim of this system is to reduce workload, and there is little need to carry out any additional assessments of most interventions because progress tracking should be related to progress in NC levels. However, if a school wants to determine the impact of the provision it has made to meet the non-academic needs of its pupils it must employ a method suitable for measuring progress in that area. Where interventions need to be measured using an alternative assessment tool the school should plan for this within the time set aside to deliver the intervention; for instance, a baseline assessment at the start of the intervention and an opportunity to carry out a final assessment at the end of the intervention period.

Some interventions have inbuilt assessment tools and it would be sensible to use these where they are provided; for instance, the commonly used physical development interventions such as BEAM (Balance, Education and Movement, a physiotherapy programme). But often the most problematic to evidence do not have a built-in assessment tool and schools need to find the simplest and most effective tool with which to measure impact. For interventions such as social skills, nurture groups, anger management, etc. the primary aim is to improve pupils' engagement with learning. In order to achieve that, Maslow's hierarchy of needs would indicate that pupils' well-being will need to be high and that too should be tracked. Some SENCOs use tools such as the Boxhall Profile for this tracking but many class teachers find it cumbersome to use and difficult to interpret. Another tool growing in popularity is the 'Scales of Well-Being and Involvement' that are part of the Experiential Education Movement. This work originated from Leuven University in Belgium under Professor Ferre Laevers (http://www.european-agency.org/agency-projects/assessment-resource-guide/documents/2008/11/Laevers.pdf). The programme includes simple scales against which teachers rank pupil well-being and levels their involvement with learning through a series of observations. They are a powerful aid to teacher self-evaluation, and measurements of both well-being and involvement pre- and post-intervention would provide the necessary evidence that progress is being made.

Many schools still assess pupils' reading age and spelling age, but although this data can be extremely useful in some instances, I would urge caution. Many of the reading age tests test reading accuracy, whereas assessment of reading within the National Curriculum is primarily an assessment of comprehension ability. If a school chooses to engage with this testing then it should select an assessment tool that measures reading comprehension age as well as reading accuracy age, and always use it alongside NC levelling.

Whatever tests or assessments are carried out, teachers should be able to use the information generated to do more than just tell what level a pupil is attaining at any given time. The assessment should also provide information about gaps in learning so that any action or intervention may be appropriately targeted and personalised.

Checklist for assessment

- Are we using reliable assessment that tells us what we need to know?
- If we use tests, are they measuring what we have taught?
- If we use teacher assessment, is it moderated regularly and are all our teachers levelling appropriately?
- Do we assess often enough and at roughly equal intervals?
- Do we baseline on entry if necessary?
- Do we use relevant assessment tools to measure impact of non-academic intervention?
- Do we use our assessments to plan for future learning, including in interventions?

Chapter 3

Data entry and analysis

However a school assesses its pupils' attainment it is the analysis of progress from one assessment to the next that is vital to determine whether action needs to be taken, and, where it has been taken, whether or not it has worked. Ofsted is clear in its view that:

> good evaluation requires systems that track progress securely towards planned outcomes and information that is used rigorously and regularly to evaluate the impact of interventions.
>
> (Ofsted 2010a, p. 14)

Within Provision Mapping the purpose of data tracking and analysis is to:

- ensure that the school can understand how well pupils are achieving over the course of a year and a Key Stage;
- swiftly identify inadequate progress and the appropriate action to address this;
- understand how successful that action has been.

The tracking of pupil progress in this way will have multiple benefits; the teacher can use it to reflect on:

- his or her quality of teaching;
- areas for self-improvement and where to ask for guidance from other colleagues;
- how to use the information to plan new strategies and improve lessons.

In addition, the senior leadership team (SLT) can use it to reflect on and identify:

- trends, by subject, class, Key Stage and vulnerable groups;
- strengths and weaknesses in practice;
- training needs and resource deployment.

The Lamb Inquiry found that in schools where pupils with learning difficulties and disabilities made outstanding progress there was a 'commitment to good or better progress for all pupils' and 'teachers who challenged themselves and scrutinised data to drive improvement' (Lamb 2009). The measurement of standards and achievement is integral to an effectively self-evaluative and successfully inclusive approach to education.

Questions that will be answered in this chapter

- Who should analyse the data and why?
- How should data be presented so that they are understood by all?
- What should the data be telling us?

Who should analyse the data and why?

A fundamentally important feature of this system is that class teachers should analyse attainment data in order to track the progress of the children in their class.

For teachers to be fully focused on the progress made by pupils in their class or group across a year they will need to be fully aware of how much progress is being made, and by whom, at each assessment point in the year. The attainment data need to be analysed by those who have taught the children and not by other members of staff such as administrators. While senior leaders will certainly need to analyse the data, we want teachers to be reflective practitioners. Analysis of data is an opportunity for them to step back from the classroom and examine the key question: who is making progress in my class? This is a fundamental process in an inclusive classroom. Engaging with pupil progress data allows teachers to consider which students are fully participating and achieving in school (Booth and Ainscow 2002), and it should be they who make the first analysis of the data and not administrators or senior staff.

I believe that the act of analysing assessment and progress data is such a vital part of a teacher's responsibility that the requirement to collate and analyse assessment data in line with school policy should be clarified in their job description. If data analysis is not carried out effectively – either the data have been incorrectly analysed or analysis is not provided within the required timescale – the teacher should be supported through the provision of training and development opportunities. Such supported development will be of particular importance under the new standards for teachers from September 2012. The DfE indicates that teachers will play a part in data analysis: 'Appropriate self-evaluation, reflection and professional development activity is critical to improving teachers' practice at all career stages' (DfE 2011b, p. 3) and is explicit in its expectations of teachers with regard to assessment.

A teacher must:

- Make accurate and productive use of assessment
- Know and understand how to assess the relevant subject and curriculum areas, including statutory assessment requirements
- Make use of formative and summative assessment to secure pupils' progress
- Use relevant data to monitor progress, set targets, and plan subsequent lessons.

(DfE 2011b, p. 6)

The introduction of the National Workload Agreement in 2003 caused some confusion among teachers as to their responsibility for the entry and management of data. The agreement had been entered into by the government and unions in an effort to ensure that both standards and teachers' work/life balance were improved (DfES 2003). However, I believe that the value of teachers entering the assessment data onto a school system is such that it should be considered the first step in effectively understanding and analysing progress. I am aware that this may not be a popular recommendation and that in so doing I risk upsetting teachers and their unions, as well as contradicting Ekins and Grimes, who previously argued:

> The inputting of data into the assessment recording system is not something that has to be done by the practitioners themselves; often it is time-consuming and can therefore effectively be completed by office administrators. We would argue that the physical activity of actually inputting data is not the key process in ensuring staff have an understanding of the data.
>
> (Ekins and Grimes 2009, p. 49)

It is my experience that in schools where the data are entered by an administrator, data manager or other member of staff and the resulting analysis presented to the teachers, there is often a lack of understanding of the analysis and there can even be a lack of ownership on the part of teachers – sometimes to such an extent that they mistrust what the data appear to be showing.

One of the key requisites for this exercise to be positive and valuable is that the system itself is manageable and easily accessible. It is no use expecting staff to carry out this task if there is only one computer in the school that has the data management system loaded onto it. Nor can there be any hope at all that staff members will be able to carry out this task if they have not received appropriate training in how to access the system.

I believe that even if they don't enter data onto a school system, at a minimum the teachers themselves should enter data into some form of analysis tool. While it is true that the entry of assessment data is time-consuming, if it is considered to be a part of the analysis process then the time is well spent. The very act of entering a grade or level will lead the teacher to consider whether that is a positive outcome or not and therefore the self-evaluative process has already begun. Ainscow (1999) argues that in order to develop more inclusive practices in schools, we need to create interruptions in teachers' thinking, encouraging them to look at the classroom from different perspectives. I believe that in an inclusive classroom we need to expect all children to be achieving as highly as they can; this is supported by recent research (e.g. Black-Hawkins *et al.* 2007). In my experience, the act of analysing the data as they are entered into the system creates just such an interruption for many teachers and enables them to ask further critical questions of their own practice and the success of classroom-based strategies to support achievement for all students.

If, therefore, the system is set up and accessible, and teachers are entering their termly assessment data onto the school's system or onto a data analysis pro-forma we can presume that the first steps towards effective analysis of data have been achieved, and we can concentrate on *how* teachers will analyse the data and present them in such a way that underachievement or inadequate progress by an individual or group can be swiftly identified.

How should data be presented so that they are understood by all?

The most important aspect of any data analysis presentation is that it is easily understood by those who need to understand it. I encourage the schools I work with to keep the presentation simple: include as much data as you need but don't overcrowd it and use visual strategies to help reinforce the information.

As stated in the introduction, there is nothing really new in this system. The origins of the data analysis pro-forma I recommend are to be found in the Improving Schools Programme (ISP) introduced to schools in 2004. This programme proposed using a tracking document to record attainment data over the course of a year that would build into a record of pupil progress. The original version was a simple grid onto which pupil names were entered but included only the attainment data for that year, no extension into P levels and no prior attainment data or targets.

Your school will undoubtedly have already developed or adapted a format for pupil progress analysis. I do not propose that you should 'reinvent the wheel' but you should consider whether the pro-forma you use contains the same information all in one place as does this pro-forma. My version retains elements of the original ISP grid but incorporates a wider range of data and targets.

As you will see from Table 3.1, this adaptation of the ISP grid enables teachers to track pupil progress across a year, from previous Key Stage and previous year-end data towards the targets set for end of year and end of Key Stage, while all the time maintaining a focus on in-year progress. For those pupils who have entered the school during the course of a Key Stage or year, prior attainment data will need to be sought from the previous school but progress can be tracked easily from their starting point or baseline.

The main purpose of entering assessment data onto such a format is so that progress can be closely monitored and any underachievement of individuals or groups swiftly identified and addressed. At any stage in the year, the teacher and the SLT should be aware of the percentage of pupils who are on track to meet their end-of-year targets. One of the ways in which this can be achieved is by the use of the visual representation of progress through a RAG (Red, Amber, Green) rating. Red would denote pupils not on track, Amber would denote pupils on track, and Green would denote pupils better than on track. RAG rating is an extremely powerful aid to self-evaluation, highlighting any inadequate progress and enabling trends to be swiftly identified. However, the criteria that will generate the RAG rating must be carefully considered and agreed, and then consistently applied by all staff prior to entry of the data onto the analysis pro-forma.

A commonly applied measure of good progress across a year between KS1 and 2 is for a pupil to make two NC sub-levels or four points' progress per year. If achieved every year that would be the same as 16 points or more than two full NC levels progress from KS1 to 2 (> 12 points progress, the government's measure of expected progress KS1 to2). Target-setting should reflect aspirational progress (usually taken from Fisher Family Trust Data) but will need to be personalised and kept constantly under review. Some pupils will need to make accelerated progress following a period of underachievement and their end-of-year targets may need to be adjusted to reflect this.

After careful consideration of how progress should be calculated I consider criteria for RAG rating (Table 3.2), where progress is expected at a rate of two sub-levels per year, to be most appropriate.

Schools need to be made aware of the pitfalls of inappropriate RAG rating. For instance, if the RAG rating is applied to the two sub-levels measure of success in its crudest form, then Amber would be applied only once the pupil had achieved two sub-levels progress. It would follow that any pupil who had not made that progress at any point during the year would be highlighted Red. One can imagine that in schools that

Table 3.1 ISP grid (adapted)

Class		Term/year								Subject	
NC level		Prior KS data	Prior year data	Assess 1	Assess 2	Assess 3	Assess 4	Assess 5	Assess 6	End year target	End KS target
Level 6	A										
	B										
	C										
Level 5	A										
	B										
	C										
Level 4	A										
	B										
	C										
Level 3	A										
	B										
	C										
Level 2	A										
	B										
	C										
Level 1	A										
	B										
	C										
P-levels	8										
	7										
	6										
	5										
	4										
% better than on track											
% on track											
% not on track											

Table 3.2 Progress RAG rating

	Assess 1	Assess 2	Assess 3	Assess 4	Assess 5	Assess 6
Negative progress	R	R	R	R	R	R
Zero progress	A	A	R	R	R	R
Plus one sub-level	G	G	A	A	R	R
Plus two sub-levels	G	G	G	G	A	A
More than two sub-levels	G	G	G	G	G	G

Key: R = Red; A = Amber; G = Green.

To access the PowerPoint presentation, as well as other eResources for this title, please go to: www.routledge.com/9780415530309

employ this method of RAG rating most if not all pupils in Terms 1 and 2 and possibly Terms 3 and 4 as well would be highlighted Red. This renders a RAG rating system almost meaningless and is a dangerous trap to fall into. If all pupils are highlighted Red because they have not yet reached their target for the year, those pupils who are falling behind or not making any progress will not stand out; they will be in danger of going undetected and opportunities to address any inadequate progress would be missed.

According to Table 3.2, there is an apparent acceptance of slow or stalled progress early on in the year but this is an acknowledgement of the frequently observed 'fall-back' over the prolonged summer break coupled with the pupils' general anxiety about transfer to a new class, Key stage or even school. However, regression at any stage in the year indicates significant issues and should be swiftly identified and addressed. The classification of Green progress throughout the year as that which is consistently above government expectations indicates the school's high expectations for its pupils. Despite the recommendation that these criteria be applied consistently, they could be personalised for individuals to address any need for accelerated progress if necessary. For those schools that are assessing pupils six times per year the criteria will remain constant over two assessments, while for those schools assessing less frequently the criteria may need to be changed, according to the key, each time the analysis is carried out. It is perfectly possible for schools to adapt their data-tracking systems to automatically RAG rate pupil progress as the data are entered, in such a way that the changing criteria are properly applied. However, I believe that the manual RAG rating of progress on a pro-forma to analyse class data delivers such a powerful reinforcement of rates of progress that it is preferable for teachers to perform this task themselves. Such action will undoubtedly increase the time it takes the teacher to enter the data onto the system or onto the data analysis sheet but it will also lead to much better analysis and self-evaluation.

What should the data be telling us?

For its analysis of school performance Ofsted relies heavily upon data published in RAISEOnline reports. However, this dataset refers to a cohort that has left the school and, while valuable in showing the outcome for groups over previous years, it cannot help to determine which pupils currently in the school need to access additional provision, nor will it help schools to evaluate the impact of that provision in enough detail or until long after it is too late to do anything about it. I therefore do not propose to spend time considering RAISEOnline reports and the information they portray but will instead focus on the analysis of in-year progress of pupils.

While there are hard facts to be gleaned from the analysis of data it will also identify questions that can only be answered by carrying out other actions such as consulting with teachers, observations of teaching, seeking the views of pupils and their parents, and making comparisons with other data such as attendance and behaviour. All of this information gathering and collaboration is necessary to obtain the full picture about pupil progress and what is enabling or preventing it.

For instance, in the illustration of a RAG-rated class dataset given in Table 3.3, we can see some interesting patterns in the progress of pupils in this class which should be giving the teacher cause for self-reflection and lead the SLT to pose certain questions. I would suggest that the clusters of pupils highlighted in Red and Green in the first assessment column would give some cause for concern. It would appear that the more able pupils have made significantly better progress than the less able. This could cause the SLT to pose some or all of the following questions, none of which can be answered without recourse to other information sources:

- Does the teacher have the ability to differentiate appropriately for the less able – or does he or she tend to concentrate on teaching the more able pupils? (Alternative evidence: observations, work scrutiny, pupil views.)
- How are additional staff deployed during lessons – is the teacher deploying the TA to support the less able in most sessions while he or she concentrates on the more able? (Alternative evidence: observations, pupil views.)
- Are the pupils making least progress accessing any additional interventions, and if so are they delivered by trained and competent staff? (Alternative evidence: Provision Maps, observations of interventions, TA skills audit.)
- Are the interventions occurring as planned or are they failing to take place because of pupil absence, lack of staff or timetable clashes? (Alternative evidence: intervention target sheets.)
- Are the least able accessing too many interventions and staying away from the classroom for too great a proportion of the day? (Alternative evidence: Provision Map, pupil views, pupil case studies.)
- Is there any correlation between poor progress and poor behaviour? Are those pupils who are making the least progress experiencing high levels of exclusion from the classroom or from school? (Alternative evidence: behaviour log, exclusions record.)
- Is there any correlation between poor progress and poor attendance? (Alternative evidence: attendance data.)
- Can the prior attainment data be relied on as accurate? (Alternative evidence: records of moderation.)
- Is the current teacher's assessment reliable? (Alternative evidence: records of moderation.)

Questions such as these should be asked whenever a number of pupils are not on track and the SLT will undoubtedly need to triangulate the information from the range of sources available to gain answers.

The teacher's RAG rating and analysis of data should provide information about the progress made by individuals but also by groups of pupils across a class. The SLT should

Table 3.3 ISP grid (adapted RAG)

Class / NC Level		Prior KS data (3)	Prior year data	Term/year — Assess 1	Assess 2	3/3 — Assess 3	Assess 4	Subject — Assess 5	Assess 6	Writing — End year Target	End KS Target
Level 6	A										
	B										
	C										
Level 5	A										
	B										
	C										
Level 4	A										AN
	B										JB, FS, DM, LV,SI
	C										WKGH,FL, HU,DH,RR
Level 3	A	AN	AN	FS,DM,AN						AN	DJ,TY,LK, PL,JJ,DE
	B	JB, FS, DM, LV,SI	JB, FS, DM, LV,SI	WK FL,HU DH,JB,SI,LV						JB, FS, DM, LV,SI	HS,TH,AWDS
	C	WKGH,FL HU,DH,RR	WKGH,FL HU,DH,RR	GH,RR,DJ, LK,						WKGH,FL, HU,DH,RR	BJ,KD,SL, CS
Level 2	A	DJ,TY,LK, PL,JJ,DE	DJ,TY,LK, PL,JJ,DE	DE, PL,HS						DJ,TY,LK, PL,JJ,DE	BC
	B	HS,TH, AWDS	HS,TH, AWDS	TY, JJ,TH						HS,TH, AWDS	
	C	BJ,KD,SL, CS	BJ,KD,SL, CS	BJ,KD,SL AW,DS						BJ,KD,SL, CS	KP (UQ)
Level 1	A	BC	BC	CS,BC						BC	KP (MQ)
	B									KP	
	C										
P-levels	8	KP	KP	KP							
	7										
	6										
	5										
	4										
% better than on track				33%							
% on track				48%							
% not on track				19%							

To access the PowerPoint presentation, as well as other eResources for this title, please go to: www.routledge.com/9780415530309

be able to combine that data analysis with analyses from other classes to build a picture of progress within a year group, a Key Stage and the school for each subject area. The combined analyses should provide the SLT with vital information about the progress of vulnerable groups and highlight any hitherto undetected vulnerable groups so that they can be prioritised for improvement.

Vulnerable groups

The analysis of vulnerable groups is a key feature of effective self-evaluation and should be the cornerstone of any school's self-review. In the first instance, data analysis can reveal which are the most vulnerable groups of pupils; which groups are making the least progress – is it free school meals (FSM), SEN school action, boys in reading? Once the most vulnerable groups have been identified, all school staff should be made aware of this analysis and which pupils belong to these groups so that action can be taken to minimise barriers to achievement. On each occasion that data are analysed, the SLT should use the class-level data about the percentage of pupils on track, the progress of the school's most vulnerable groups should be considered and the impact of any action taken reviewed. For instance, if a school has purchased additional literature to stimulate boys' reading is there corresponding progress in those boys' reading?

In brief, the school's SLT should be able to use the data analysis to find out the following school-level information:

- the proportion of pupils who are not on track, on track or better than on track to achieve their end-of-year targets in reading, writing and maths;
- whether there are any class, year, Key Stage or subject-specific progress issues;
- whether there is any pattern or trend in progress of vulnerable groups;
- whether interventions have had an impact on progress.

Such cumulative school data could be presented in tabular form (see Table 3.4).

The school would need to identify its most vulnerable groups and filter the data for the percentage better than on track, on track or not on track of each of these groups by class. The data for the vulnerable groups could be compared with that of all pupils in each class to ascertain where there are gaps in performance and where action needs to be taken to close these gaps. This exercise could be further refined and improved if, instead of comparison against all pupils, the vulnerable group were compared with the inverse group, for instance, FSM against non-FSM, SEN against non-SEN.

As pupil premium becomes a feature of school budgets the impact of this financial resource will also need to be closely tracked and monitored. The government has stated that from September 2012 schools will be expected to report on its website how this money is being spent and its impact (The School Information (England) (Amendments) Regulations 2012). There will also be information about the impact of pupil premium in a school's RAISEOnline report. Monitoring of impact will vary according to the type of provision made; for instance, if a school identifies that a large proportion of FSM pupils have poor attendance it may choose to employ a family liaison officer. The cost of this could be met fully, or in part, from the pupil premium. A measure of the impact of this intervention would be that attendance for the FSM group would increase substantially and outcomes improve (see Table 3.5). Monitoring at group level is essential but schools that have a low percentage of pupils in receipt of the pupil premium may decide to

Table 3.4 Vulnerable groups analysis

Analysis of class data																			Date:
SUBJECT																			
Vulnerable group 1																			
Vulnerable group 2																			
Vulnerable group 3																			
	Year 1			Year 2			Year 3			Year 4			Year 5			Year 6			
	1	3	5	1	3	5	1	3	5	1	3	5	1	3	5	1	3	5	
Assessment by end of term																			
% and number of:																			
all pupils better than on track																			
all pupils on track																			
all pupils not on track																			
VG1 better than on track																			
VG1 on track																			
VG1 not on track																			
VG2 better than on track																			
VG2 on track																			
VG2 not on track																			
VG3 better than on track																			
VG3 on track																			
VG3 not on track																			

Progress	Better than on track	On track	Not on track
Term 1	+ve	same	-ve
Term 3	++ve	+ve	same or -ve
Term 5	+++ve	++ve	+ve, same or -ve

Table 3.5 Pupil premium: analysis of spending and impact

	% LAC	% FSM	% Services	Total pupil premium as % of school roll	Total funding	Pupil premium/non pupil premium (% making better than expected progress in English)	Pupil premium/non pupil premium (% making better than expected progress in maths)	Pupil premium/non pupil premium average attendance	Pupil premium/non pupil premium behaviour (no. of incidents)	Pupil premium/non pupil premium behaviour (no. of exclusions – pupils)	Other/enrichment
Pupil premium 2011–12	5%	27%	0	32%	£27,400	13%/41%	24%/36%	84%/97%	72/85	15/7	
Action funded or part funded by pupil premium						Phonic programme paired reading learning mentor £15,000	Numbers count £2000 training + £3000 delivery	FLO £7000		FLO	Music lessons x 2 Football strip funding £400
Impact						Increase of 5% in % of PP making better than expected progress	Increase of 14% in % of PP making better than expected progress	Average PP attendance +4% Persistent non-attenders reducing		No. of exclusions for PP group remains high	Increased engagement

Table 3.6 Pupil premium progress and tracking

Pupil premium analysis by term/year (pupil premium spending highlighted)

Pupil	Year/class	Type	SEN	Intervention	Reading entry	Exit	Writing entry	Exit	Maths entry	Exit	Behaviour entry	Exit	Attendance entry	Exit	Other	Impact
Joe Bloggs	2/ Robins	FSM	n/a	Reading FLO Parenting	1c	1b	1c	1c	1b	2c	n/a	n/a	89%	95%		Positive
Mary Smith	3/ Swallows	LAC	SA+	Reading Writing Maths Social skills	P7	P8	P7	P7	P8	P7	5 incidents recorded 1 x 2 day exclusion	3 incidents recorded No exclusions	100%	100%		Positive

evaluate the impact of this intervention upon individuals and could represent this in tabular form (Table 3.6). Reporting on outcomes for pupil premium pupils on the school's website must be carefully composed to avoid any pupil identification.

The analysis of data is a critical feature of this Provision Mapping system but it is only a starting point. *The Improving Schools Programme Handbook* (DCSF 2009) reinforced the fact that data analysis should be a starting point for discussion about the causes of underachievement. It is the discussion and subsequent action that is key to the success of this system in improving outcomes – no matter how well we assess pupils or how well we analyse the assessment data, outcomes will not improve unless we do something with what we have found out.

Checklist for data analysis

- Are class teachers entering and analysing class-level assessment data?
- Do class teachers use a RAG rating system consistently to highlight any inadequate progress?
- Are class teachers using this analysis of data to prompt rigorous self-review?
- Is the SLT making appropriate and useful school-level analyses of progress; in particular the progress of vulnerable groups?
- Are links being made between different datasets: records of observation, pupil views, attendance and behaviour?
- Are all staff members aware of the most vulnerable groups in the school and are they making the necessary adaptations to their teaching?

Chapter 4

Pupil progress review meetings

The Ofsted review of SEN and disability reported that:

> Inspectors saw the similar needs of different children being met effectively in a wide range of different ways. However, what consistently worked best was a close analysis of their needs, often as they changed and developed, matched to a clear view of the impact of intervention on outcomes for them.
>
> (Ofsted 2010c, p. 10)

In order to achieve the above, a school will need to establish a system that has structured opportunities for frequent and regular analysis and review built into it. In most schools such opportunities are already established and take the form of pupil progress review meetings, adapted from the ISP programme. Much has been written about these meetings and how they should be conducted. In many schools they are firmly embedded in the annual calendar, but I have often found that the best use is not made of these meetings; they can lack focus and are sometimes carried out in isolation from other school processes – conversations about progress that do not lead to any adjustment of practice or provision.

Reflection on progress needs to be rigorous. Howes and colleagues (2009) found that discussion or reflection on inclusion can sometimes reinforce inappropriate action. How many schools still deliver a programme or intervention that they have been using for years simply because they have that programme and the people trained to deliver it? How many of those programmes are dropped when it is shown that they have little or no impact? How many pupil progress review meetings actually bring about such change? In order to ensure that change happens there needs to be a structure to enable reflection and discussion on progress and this can be achieved through pupil progress review meetings, but they must be strongly led and given high priority. Returning to the diet analogy, the component of the Weight Watchers programme that is different from ordinary dieting is the group aspect; the coming together of dieters to measure progress and reflect on strategies or interventions that work and achieve weight loss effectively. The pupil progress review meeting is the group aspect of this Provision Mapping system.

The format for pupil progress review meetings was clearly set out in *The Improving Schools Programme Handbook*:

At pupil progress meetings teachers share their evidence of the progress that children have made; they identify what has supported children's learning and what has got in the way. They decide upon the next steps to support children's progress.

(DCSF 2009, p. 46)

It is clear that the main aim should be to review progress and agree action to address any identified issues. It is also clear that it is teachers who are expected to drive the meetings and for this they will need to be well prepared by thoroughly analysing their assessment data. Such action will reinforce their responsibility for the progress and outcomes of all pupils in their class, including those with SEN or disability. It should be the class teacher, not the SENCO, who identifies the children who need to receive additional intervention, sets the targets for the interventions, evaluates their effectiveness and proposes that further or different action should be taken if an intervention has not brought about accelerated progress.

In brief, pupil progress meetings should be structured, professional conversations that lead to strategic decision-making and effect change to improve pupil outcomes.

Questions that will be answered in this chapter

- When should pupil progress meetings take place?
- How often should they take place?
- Who should be involved?
- How should staff prepare for pupil progress review meetings?
- What should the meeting look like?
- What should pupil progress meetings achieve?

When should pupil progress meetings take place?

The meetings should generally be timetabled to take place in the week following assessment and data analysis. They need to take place as soon after assessment as possible so that the data being considered are the most current. They should not be planned to take place after school or at lunch or break times – this is such an important aspect of the strategic management of the school that it should be timetabled into the school week, cover arranged and staff given full opportunity to make the best use of the time. Most schools devote an hour per class, and if staff prepare well for the meeting that amount of time should be sufficient.

How often should the meetings take place?

I believe that schools which assess and review with different frequency can be equally successful and each school will need to reflect on the pattern that would be most appropriate. If we are looking for two NC sub-levels of progress for most pupils over the course of one year, in a system that assesses pupils six times per year we would not be able to detect measureable progress each time an assessment is carried out. It is sensible to assess six times and review six times per year to ensure that action swiftly follows on from any identification of need, but schools must beware of falling into the trap of accepting no progress too often. For instance, if you are not expecting to see progress at each review, when does no progress finally become unacceptable?

Some schools that assess six times per year only meet to discuss pupil progress three times per year. This method allows them to regularly measure attainment and update their progress grids, but only formally review progress over intervals at which it should be discernible. While reviewing progress three times a year would mean that almost every time progress is reviewed there would be an expectation that some measureable progress could be observed, it does mean that issues of regressive progress are not addressed through pupil progress review swiftly enough.

Some schools both measure attainment and review progress three or four times per year and are confident that this level of frequency is sufficient to enable them to make the changes to practice that are necessary to secure improvement. Personal experience leads me to believe that the best model (though admittedly the most time-consuming) is to assess six times a year and review six times a year. However, it is also perfectly acceptable to assess six times a year and review four times, the first at the end of term 1, the second at the end of term 3, the third in term 5 and the fourth and final review taking place at the end of term 6 so that it can be aligned with transition and informing parents through reports. This model also means that a new Provision Map can be drafted for the start of the next academic year so that interventions can commence early and no time is wasted. This can be seen in Table 4.1.

Who should be involved?

The pupil progress review meeting is an informed professional dialogue between the class teacher, a member of the SLT (where possible the HT) and the SENCO. Other staff may be included in the meeting such as support staff, year or Key Stage coordinators, etc., but schools should be aware of the difficulties of keeping discussion focused and succinct when too many people are present. Some schools employ SENCOs part-time or have SENCOs with a high teaching commitment. In these schools there will have to be a degree of flexibility, and possibly additional expense incurred to ensure that the SENCO can be present at each pupil progress meeting. The presence of the SENCO is necessary to help teachers select the most appropriate method of support and to advise on the strategies and interventions that should be most effective. If they are not able to be present

Table 4.1 PPM timetable

Model	Term 1	Term 2	Term 3	Term 4	Term 5	Term 6
Six + six times per	Assess Data analysis PPM	Assess Data analysis PPM	Assess Data analysis PPM	Assess Data analysis PPM	Assess Data analysis PPM	Assess Data analysis PPM
Six + four times per year	Assess Data analysis PPM	Assess Data analysis	Assess Data analysis PPM	Assess Data analysis	Assess Data analysis PPM	Assess Data analysis PPM
Three + three times per year	Assess Data analysis PPM		Assess Data analysis PPM		Assess Data analysis PPM	

some of the benefits of this system will be lost. There would then need to be a second meeting between the teacher and the SENCO to discuss the proposed provision and possibly yet another meeting between the SLT member and the SENCO to discuss issues around pupil progress in interventions. Additional meetings should be avoided at all costs – it is far better to have everyone present at the one meeting.

How should staff prepare for the meetings?

The key to the success of these meetings is in the quality of the preparation. Meetings that take place when the teacher and/or the SLT are unprepared will naturally be less effective. I have attended meetings where data have not been analysed prior to the meetings and trying to carry out that level of analysis during the meeting means that there is no time to move on to discuss provision. In order to ensure that the meetings are as efficient and effective as possible, schools should provide staff with clear guidelines. *The Improving Schools Programme Handbook* lists the features of an effective pupil progress review meeting:

> Pupil progress meetings:
> *   take place on a termly or half-termly basis;
> *   are based on the information that the teacher has about the children's progress over the term or half-term;
> *   use the full range of assessment information from day-to-day, periodic and transitional assessments;
> *   can include evidence from children about their learning;
> *   are a dialogue between teachers and the senior leadership team about what has worked and what needs to change to support the children's learning;
> *   plan and record the next steps for the school to take (in class and beyond) to meet the children's needs;
> *   are professional learning for teachers, as the discussion and challenge helps them to reflect on and evaluate the impact of their teaching;
> *   help leadership teams to pinpoint the needs of underperforming groups across the school, or an area of the curriculum that would benefit from whole-school CPD;
> *   provide detailed evidence to support discussions with parents about their children's learning.
>
> (DCSF 2009)

I have included this list, as I believe the features of a successful pupil progress meeting remain the same now as they were when this programme was first rolled out, with one exception: the eagle-eyed ISP devotee will note that I have removed the reference to the tracking of a target group:

> *   focus particularly on those children who have previously been identified as needing to make accelerated progress (the target group) and those children who have made more or less progress than expected.
>
> (DCSF 2009, p. 46)

I have found that this guidance has often been very misleading. I propose that the focus be on the progress of *all* students and not on 'target groups', as I have observed that in schools that have adopted the target group principle, *only* the target group is discussed during the meeting, and the group selected at the start of the year to be the target group has quickly become inappropriate yet has often gone unchanged, meaning that more vulnerable pupils have not been identified or properly supported over the course of a year.

Although these are the key features of a pupil progress meeting, they are not very directive and I believe schools should set clear guidelines for staff on how to prepare for the meetings. This guidance could form part of a school's teaching and learning policy. For instance:

- All teachers will complete their analysis of pupil progress and provide the SLT with a copy of the analysis in the week prior to the meetings.
- The SLT will consider all the data analyses and prepare questions on pupil performance to be discussed during the review meeting.
- Teachers will consider which teaching (Wave 1) strategies have been successful and why, as well as those that have been less successful, and be prepared to discuss this.
- The impact of any intervention undertaken since the last pupil progress meeting will be measured by teachers and recorded on the class Provision Map (see Chapter 5).
- Teachers will consider which pupils are in need of additional intervention in the coming term, decide what form that should take and draft a new class Provision Map (see Chapter 5).

In many schools there has been an expectation that staff would prepare for these meetings by compiling statements on the barriers to learning for each pupil. This practice was also proposed as part of the Improving Schools Programme with pro-formas for recording the barriers provided. Although I agree that the act of identifying barriers can be a valuable one, it will only fit in with my suggested model of pupil progress review meetings if the discussion during the meeting does not linger on the barriers themselves, nor are teachers tempted to cite the barriers as reasons why pupils (particularly those with SEN) *cannot* make good or accelerated progress. I am concerned that the practice of identifying barriers leads to an overemphasis on reasons why the pupil cannot make progress and not on what action the school can take to secure that progress.

Although I urge caution in focusing on barriers to learning in pupil progress review meetings, all schools have a number of pupils who have significant barriers to learning that may be related to any one of the many reasons for vulnerability: SEN or disability, poverty, family breakdown, social situation, etc. These pupils will have needs that can change on a daily basis and should be very closely monitored. All staff in the school need to be made aware of any change in circumstances and therefore the school should devise a way of regularly updating its staff. One way is to create a vulnerable pupil or V register. This would be a list of the most vulnerable pupils and could be a standing agenda item at every staff meeting. It would not take long to mention briefly that a child's parents had finally split up, that another child is temporarily living with grandparents, that another has experienced bereavement or been in hospital, and so on. All of this can be communicated electronically but my experience of that method is that no school can rely on its entire staff to keep themselves abreast of any changes in this way. Weekly updates at staff meetings not only alert all staff members to changes but permit brief discussion on how to address these issues. For example: should we mention the bereavement; should we communicate with both grandparents and parents; has there been any achievement that we could use to raise self-esteem – moving up a level in reading, for instance. For those pupils who are extremely vulnerable there may occasionally be a need for daily updates which could be part of a morning briefing in schools. Schools that have introduced this practice have found that it has enhanced the way their most vulnerable pupils are supported and ensured that swift and appropriate action is taken where necessary without the need to wait for the next pupil progress meeting.

What should the meeting look like?

I am often asked what a good pupil progress review meeting looks like. I think it is helpful to think of the meeting in sections.

Part 1

The first part of the conversation (about 20 per cent) should be centred on the review with some key questions:

- Who has made good progress, and who has not?
- Are there are any groups that have performed better than others?
- Are there any other factors such as attendance and behaviour that need to be taken into account?

If teachers know that only 20 per cent of the time will be devoted to this area, it may help them to understand the importance of carrying out a full analysis in advance of the meeting.

Part 2

In order to maximise impact, the majority of the time in the meeting should be spent on answering the 'so what are we going to do about it?' question. The discussion about what action to take is critical and should be focused primarily on what adjustments need to be made to classroom teaching. This should include:

- a review of the strategies that have proved successful as well as those that have not;
- whether there are any different strategies that could be used;
- if necessary, where the teacher could go to for support or training.

The aim is that teachers will have spent some time considering their own strengths and weaknesses and should come to the meeting prepared to share this information so that their strengths can be disseminated and their weaknesses addressed and improved. If teachers have not been able to self-reflect in this way, the SLT should use the information they have about the quality of teaching alongside the analysis of pupil progress and evaluation of interventions and may need to engage in a robust conversation around improvement (see Chapter 7). If the SLT considers that there may need to be a conversation of this nature, it would be even more important to keep the number of people who attend the meeting to a minimum so that any issues of competency are discussed in such a way that confidentiality can be maintained. In the SEN review Ofsted endorses this emphasis on the need for quality in whole-class teaching rather than additional intervention:

> Inspectors observed schools focusing on providing additional help for pupils with identified special educational needs rather than on improving the quality of their standard offer for all pupils. In some of their visits to schools, inspectors met pupils who were provided with significant additional support whose needs could and should have been met by appropriately differentiated teaching, good learning and pastoral support earlier on.
>
> (Ofsted 2010c, p. 22)

In total, the discussion about teaching strategies should take up a further 40 per cent of the meeting time.

Part 3

Only once the discussion about classroom teaching strategies has concluded should there be any discussion about interventions. This section will absorb the final 40 per cent of the meeting time. Again, the meeting will be expedited by good preparation on the part of the teachers who should have evaluated the impact of the interventions on the Provision Map prior to the meeting. The following questions could then be posed:

- What does the evaluated Provision Map tell us works best?
- Should any interventions be continued?
- Should any interventions be ceased or replaced with something more effective?

The decision about who should access which intervention will, for the most part, be arrived at through scrutiny of the academic progress data. Some pupils need support in non-academic areas and this may involve scrutiny of attendance and/or behaviour data or information on social or emotional difficulties, for instance, data from the Leuven Scales of well-being and involvement. Any decisions taken about additional interventions should also include the targets that should be set for each intervention, and the timescale, the person to deliver it, grouping and strategies or programmes to be used agreed. All of this information can be recorded on the draft class Provision Map prior to the meeting and updated and agreed during the meeting (see Chapter 5).

Final progress meetings: transition

The final pupil progress review meeting of the year should be a transition meeting. It would be sensible to ensure that teachers from both the current class and the next class are involved in the review meeting so that the new teacher can be apprised of the range of needs in the class and the interventions and strategies that have been successful in meeting those needs. Again this will reduce the number of meetings in a school if the pupil progress review meeting and the transition meeting are combined. It also means that the two teachers can work together to plan a draft Provision Map for the new class and that intervention can commence as soon as the new school year starts.

What should pupil progress meetings achieve?

Enhanced reflection and self-evaluation

The pupil progress review meeting should be a positive experience for all involved. It should support a school culture of self-evaluation and review, and should aim to acknowledge and celebrate achievement as well as offer challenge. It should be a route to disseminating good practice as well as a tool for identifying and tackling practice that is inadequate. Where pupil progress review meetings work best, staff are well prepared and welcome the opportunity to problem-solve with colleagues. These meetings must be strategic – they must lead to a change in practice that will secure improved outcomes.

Improved whole-class teaching and additional intervention

The main objective of pupil progress meetings should be to ensure that good whole-class teaching is in place and that pupils in the class are making good progress. If the teaching needs to be improved or if good teaching is in place but is not sufficient to secure good progress and attainment, additional action must be taken. Where the class teaching is found to be less than good, the action should be primarily directed at improving the whole-class teaching and should not result in increased provision for pupils away from the classroom – every effort should be made to reduce this additional and different intervention to the minimum necessary to secure improvement. If the teaching is good and the majority of pupils make good progress, the objective should be to provide appropriate additional intervention for those for whom good teaching is not enough.

Links to whole-school processes

In order to achieve this the SLT needs to make links to such processes as performance management, staff development and training, staff deployment, prioritisation of spending on resources and school development planning. The class data analyses should be collated and considered at a whole-school level so that any cohort, year, class or vulnerable group issues can be identified. Previously identified vulnerable groups should be tracked and the impact of any additional interventions calculated at a group and individual level. This action will be discussed in more detail in Chapter 5.

A further outcome of the pupil progress review is that staff may need to be deployed differently, which could have a performance management implication and will certainly necessitate some induction and support. A re-prioritisation of resources should be another outcome of a successful pupil progress review cycle; the SLT will be able to determine where there is a need for extra resourcing or staffing. For instance, a group of under-achieving ASD pupils may indicate a need to deploy an ASD-trained TA to that class. Any significant re-prioritisation or resourcing, including training, should be reflected in the school's self-evaluation and development plan.

Provision Mapping

The drafting of a new Provision Map is a key outcome of the pupil progress review discussion. The selection of intervention should be arrived at by considering what has worked well previously or, if a new intervention is necessary, national or local research will need to be considered. Ofsted recommends its inspectors consider the information about the impact of interventions presented in the Toolkit of Strategies to Improve Learning (Higgins *et al.* 2011) and schools too could use this evidence base to support decision-making. I do not intend to recommend any specific interventions here as the list is endless, but the key principles for the delivery of successful intervention are the same whichever intervention is selected: that it should have appropriately trained staff, appropriate frequency and duration of delivery, clear understanding of targets and purpose, and adherence to the programme.

Checklist for pupil progress review meetings

- Are the meetings timetabled to take place immediately following in-class assessment?
- Are the class teachers following the school's policy on preparation for these meetings? Has the SLT been provided with class-level data analyses and corresponding evaluated class Provision Maps prior to the meeting?
- Is the SLT fully prepared for each meeting?
- Do the meetings focus on how to improve whole-class teaching?
- Does the SENCO attend each of the meetings?
- Is the evaluated class Provision Map discussed and does the school have a clear picture of 'what works'?
- As an outcome of the meeting does each class have a new Provision Map listing effective teaching strategies and details of additional intervention?
- Are links made between the outcome of the meetings and performance management, self-evaluation and school development planning?

Chapter 5

Provision Maps

The key to making this system work is the Provision Map.

In the Weight Watchers analogy, the Provision Map is the Weight Watchers book or record of weight loss (or gain), a record of the target to be achieved and a place for notes to inform future dieting or exercise practice. The recording of progress alongside ideas of new strategies to use helps focus the user on the progress that needs to be made and how that could be best achieved. If the contents of the book are shared more widely the dieter has more chance of keeping to the diet and achieving the target.

Although, strictly speaking, the Provision Map is nothing more than a management tool, in the format detailed here it will be evaluative and can link several school processes together. It may be used to aid planning and target-setting, and can also help staff to monitor the amount of time pupils spend away from the classroom on intervention programmes. Collated and evaluated Provision Maps can provide evidence on the impact of interventions for the school's self-evaluation and can be shared with parents so that they better understand the provision being made for their child and the ways they can help at home.

Instead of taking minutes of the pupil progress review meeting (which generates paperwork), the actions agreed at the meeting can be recorded onto the draft version of the Provision Map for the coming term created by the class teacher and discussed during the meeting. This ensures that all will be agreed on the way that action should be prioritised, the targets for any intervention and the staff and resources involved.

Questions that will be answered in this chapter

- Why do schools need a Provision Map?
- What should a Provision Map look like?
- How do we draft, maintain and evaluate a Provision Map?
- What is the SENCO's role in Provision Mapping?

Why do schools need a Provision Map?

Ofsted's SEN and disability review in 2010 found that effective schools had:

- high aspirations for the achievement of all children and young people;
- good teaching and learning for all children and young people;
- provision based on careful analysis of need, close monitoring of each individual's progress and a shared perception of desired outcomes;
- evaluated the effectiveness of provision at all levels in helping to improve opportunities and progress;
- leaders who looked to improving general provision to meet a wider range of needs rather than always increasing additional provision.

(Ofsted 2010c, p. 31)

If a school adopts the system described in this book then it will certainly ensure that all these aspects of an effective approach to meeting pupils' needs will be in place and can be sustained and improved upon. The Provision Map, if used properly, will act as a stimulus for change:

- to ensure that targets are aspirational enough;
- as a prompt to remind teachers of effective strategies to support the most vulnerable pupils;
- as a record of the progress made in interventions and the effectiveness of each;
- as a communication aid with both parents and other agencies.

It is my experience that when schools start to use Provision Maps to detail provision, the conversations that are held about how to address inadequate progress often lead to a reduction in the number of interventions as teachers are better supported to improve classroom teaching and they become less inclined to release pupils for intervention programmes (see Chapter 7).

In the SEN review Ofsted recorded examples of local authorities and schools using Provision Mapping to improve provision and outcomes for children and young people with additional needs. They defined Provision Mapping as 'an audit of how well planned interventions meet needs; it also identifies any gaps in provision' (Ofsted 2010c, p. 63):

The best Provision Mapping observed did not simply list what was available; it also showed which interventions were particularly effective. This contributed to efficient planning to meet the needs of individuals or groups, kept pupils and their parents up to date with progress following an intervention, and helped a school or a local authority to evaluate its overall effectiveness, as illustrated below.

1   The local authority had prepared a simple electronic 'provision mapping' tool that was used by all its schools. This enabled the schools to keep, in one place, details of all the provision they made for pupils with special educational needs and/or disabilities. The resources in terms of staff, time and equipment and costs were included. The system automatically kept an account of ongoing expenditure against the school's annual budget for special needs. This provision map linked directly to the individual targets for each pupil and to the school's tracking system. The impact of support could therefore be monitored and evaluated effectively, and changes to provision made on the basis of robust evidence.

2   The local authority expected schools to do this analysis formally and in depth at least twice a year, in addition to the usual continuing monitoring of all pupils. A new extension to the programme was to make it even easier for the school to analyse the progress of groups of pupils who were receiving different types of provision, for example all those in Year 7 who attended a support class for their reading.

This type of tool improved accountability and provided greater openness, but it was seen infrequently across the sample.

(Ofsted 2010c, pp. 63–64)

The use of Provision Maps as described in this book has evolved from earlier models (Gross and White 2003; Ekins and Grimes 2009). However, the version of a Provision Map that I propose would not be costed as suggested by Gross and White and Ofsted in the model described above. Unlike Ekins and Grimes' model, it would be evaluated and it would be updated more frequently than twice a year as suggested by Ofsted and three times a year as suggested by Ekins and Grimes. It would be linked to the monitoring of all pupils, not just SEN pupils, and would lead to provision for any pupil that needed it, rather than just for SEN pupils. The Ofsted review recognised the evaluative potential of Provision Maps and that this could be conducted at an individual and group level, but it also appeared to link this evaluation to the costing of interventions, something I do not consider appropriate or advisable, as it could lead to cessation of an intervention because of expense, irrespective of effectiveness.

What should a Provision Map look like?

As with the data analysis sheets, Provision Maps need to be easily understood by all those who need to use them: teachers, support staff, supply teachers, senior leadership teams and parents. Schools may choose to present them in a different format or add additional information, but the key elements of a Provision Map should be the same for any school:

- Name of class and date.
- Record of class-specific quality teaching strategies (Wave 1).
- Details of targeted or personalised support, to include:
  - name of pupil
  - title of intervention
  - length, duration and frequency of sessions
  - person delivering intervention
  - entry data
  - target
  - exit data
  - outcome.

The pro-forma shown in Table 5.1 may be used in any primary school. It can be expanded to include as many interventions as necessary and stored electronically so that all school users can have access to it, and it can be updated easily when necessary.

The term in which it was composed should be recorded on each draft of a Provision Map so that progress over time can be evidenced (Table 5.2).

Table 5.1 Provision Map

Year: Date: Term:

Quality teaching strategies:

Interventions:

Intervention	Group size	Frequency/ duration/staff	Pupil	Entry data	Intervention target	Exit data	Outcome

Table 5.2 Provision Map

Year 4	Date:	Term 4						
Quality teaching strategies:								
Interventions:								
Intervention	Group size	Frequency/ duration/staff	Pupil	Entry data	Intervention target	Exit data	Outcome	

The first section of the class Provision Map should list the effective, whole-class quality teaching strategies in place for that class at that time (Table 5.3). This is a critical element of a class Provision Map and is discussed in greater detail in Chapter 7.

The remainder of the Provision Map is concerned with additional interventions, the pupils accessing them, their frequency and duration, their entry and exit data and targets, and, ultimately, their evaluation.

How should schools draft, maintain and evaluate the Provision Map?

The class teacher is the person responsible for the class Provision Map and it is they who should draft, maintain and evaluate it. This system aims to increase the responsibility of class teachers for all pupils in their class at all times – including when they are absent from the classroom attending additional intervention. Ofsted expects teachers to retain this responsibility and to be able to demonstrate that they have an understanding of the impact of the intervention upon progress (Ofsted Training for Inspectors, January 2012).

The draft Provision Map

Following in-class assessment of all pupils, the gathering of pupil views and analysis of the data, the class teacher should have a very clear idea of who needs additional intervention in order to make better progress. The class teacher should consider both the interventions that would be most effective to redress any inadequate progress and the pupils who need to access them, and from this create a draft version of the class Provision Map for the coming term.

Each intervention should have the name of the pupils and their entry data taken from the class assessment. For those interventions where classroom assessments are not the most appropriate assessment tool, the teacher should identify the best way to measure impact and carry out a suitable baseline assessment at the start of the intervention programme. In addition, each intervention should have the timing, frequency and duration determined along with the person who will deliver it and the target to be achieved.

As you will see from this draft version of a class Provision Map (Table 5.4), the teacher has entered the groups and interventions proposed for the coming term. Entry or baseline data has been entered alongside pupil names. Targets have been considered and written onto the Provision Map. The group size has been entered (important if pupils are being drawn from more than one class for interventions), as has the timing, frequency, duration and the person delivering the intervention. This particular feature of the Provision Map enables the teacher or SENCO to calculate the time a pupil spends away from the classroom (Table 5.5).

I have often found this to be extremely valuable. In one school I used the Provision Map to track an individual pupil selected at random. The child was absent from the classroom for a total of five hours per week. The length of time he was absent from the classroom never exceeded 20 minutes and I estimated that he must be absent for a part of nearly every lesson. When asked about his behaviour it was little surprise to hear that he found it difficult to settle and concentrate in lessons. Teachers must reflect on the total length of time their pupils are absent from lessons and ensure that any absence from the classroom is absolutely essential.

Table 5.3 Provision Map

Year 4	Date:			Term 4				
Quality teaching strategies: visual timetable, task boards x 5, peer mentoring, grouping for support, cumulative reward system, writing frames, word banks, feelings wall, worry box, phone-a-friend, wobble seats x 3.								
Interventions:								
Intervention	Group size	Frequency/ duration/staff	Pupil	Entry data	Intervention target	Exit data	Outcome	

Table 5.4 Provision Map (draft)

Year 4	Date:	Term 4

Quality teaching strategies: visual timetable, task boards x 5, peer mentoring, grouping for support, cumulative reward system, writing frames, word banks, feelings wall, worry box, phone-a-friend, wobble seats x 3.

Interventions:

Intervention	Group size	Frequency/ duration/staff	Pupil	Entry data	Intervention target	Exit data	Outcome
Comprehension group	1:6	3 x 15 x 6 weeks HLTA	Amy Joe Dan Fred Bob Max	2c 2b 2c 2c 2b 2c	Plus one sub-level To use expression in reading To demonstrate understanding of text in conversation		
Numeracy	1:6	4 x 20 x 6 weeks (early am) HLTA	Dan Fred Carl Amy Jane Sara	3c 3c 3b 3c 3c 3c	Plus one sub-level To be able to use multiplication facts (2, 5 and 10) confidently To use the 24-hour clock		
Paired reading	1:1	Daily, x 10, HLTA	Joe	2b	To re-engage with text Read with expression		
Social skills	1:3	3 x 15	Carl Jack Wayne	Leuven targets 1 2 4 2 3 2	To work on independent Organisational skills Working with others Working with others		

Table 5.5 Provision Map (draft)

Year 4	Date:	Term 4

Quality teaching strategies: visual timetable, task boards × 5, peer mentoring, grouping for support, cumulative reward system, writing frames, word banks, feelings wall, worry box, phone-a-friend, wobble seats × 3.

Interventions:

Intervention	Group size	Frequency/ duration/staff	Pupil	Entry data	Intervention target	Exit data	Outcome
Comprehension group	1:6	3 × 15 × 6 weeks HLTA	Amy Joe Dan Fred Bob Max	2c 2b 2c 2c 2b 2c	Plus one sub-level To use expression in reading To demonstrate understanding of text in conversation		
Numeracy	1:6	4 × 20 × 6 weeks (early am) HLTA	Dan Fred Carl Amy Jane Sara	3c 3c 3b 3c 3c 3c	Plus one sub-level To be able to use multiplication facts (2, 5 and 10) confidently To use the 24-hour clock		
Paired reading	1:1	Daily, × 10, HLTA	Joe	2b	To re-engage with text Read with expression		
Social skills	1:3	3 × 15	Carl Jack Wayne	Leuven targets 1 2 4 2 3 2	To work on independent Organisational skills Working with others Working with others		

In another school class teachers reported during pupil progress review meetings that they had great difficulty meeting the needs of pupils who had been absent for part of a lesson and who returned to the classroom mid-session. They reported that a number of pupils were anxious about rejoining a lesson and the teachers lamented that they could not always give sufficient or immediate attention to the pupil. Two solutions became apparent: to make sure that, where appropriate, intervention session length would match lesson length but when this was not appropriate the school would ensure that the member of staff delivering the intervention would be timetabled to accompany the child or group back to the classroom and settle them to the task before moving on. The Provision Map column detailing timing, frequency and duration was used to support the teachers' planning for such action and to ensure that the timetabling of staff was adjusted appropriately.

At this draft stage all entries on the Provision Map are subject to change and can be adjusted at the pupil progress review meeting. *The targets for each intervention are a critical feature of the class Provision Map.* It is this target-setting, along with the entry and exit data that replace the need for IEPs for the great majority of pupils, which reduces bureaucracy. Such intervention targets on a Provision Map must be SMART (Specific, Measureable, Attainable, Relevant and Timed).

- **Specific**: The class teacher will have devised targets that relate to either gaps in learning or to developing skills hitherto undeveloped. The targets must be more than just 'plus one sub-level' and should include the specific aspects of learning that have been identified. For instance, plus one sub-level and to be able to use number bonds to ten in problem-solving.
- **Measureable**: They are accompanied by entry and exit data.
- **Attainable** (but also **Aspirational**): Attainable should, in my view, be joined by Aspirational as I would expect that these targets would be highly aspirational. Many schools question the validity of setting a target of a sub-level progress in six weeks of intervention but I would argue that if pupil progress has been stalled, or even regressed, then accelerated progress must be swiftly achieved. If the school is going to invest in additional intervention it must get value for money – the measure of which would be accelerated progress.
- **Relevant**: The class teacher will have set the targets from a gap analysis and from what is known about the child as well as with regard to current in-class targets and aspects to be covered in schemes of work.
- **Timed**: They will have clear timing, frequency and duration marked on the Provision Map.

Ofsted noted that IEPs were seldom effective in securing progress:

Inspectors found that the challenge represented by the targets in the individual education plans scrutinised was highly variable' and 'outcomes for all children or young people were still, or until very recently had been, evaluated only in terms of whether they had met the targets on their individual education plan'.

(Ofsted 2010c, p. 64)

The need to make targets more measurable in order to impact upon progress has been endorsed by the government which has indicated an intention to remove advice on IEPs and encourage schools to explore the ways in which the bureaucratic burden could be reduced through new approaches to planning, reviewing and tracking the progress of all pupils (DfE 2011b, p. 98).

The intervention targets on the Provision Map may be used not only to detail the aims of the intervention, but also to support the performance management process for teaching assistants. It is important here to consider how TAs are deployed in this system. In most schools, interventions are delivered by support staff, the majority of whom are attached to classes. They will be expected to cover the whole range of interventions from speech and language to numeracy and literacy as well as social skills, etc. for the class to which they are deployed. Many schools report that their teachers want a class-based TA working alongside them in the classroom but there is no evidence to support the impact of such practice upon pupil progress (Blatchford *et al.* 2009; Higgins *et al.* 2011), and Ofsted reported 'High-quality intervention from members of the wider workforce who had qualifications and training that were directly relevant to the specific areas in which they were working had the greatest impact on learning' (Ofsted 2010c, p. 5). All classes will have different needs, and it is unlikely that all support staff would have the skills necessary to deliver such a wide range of interventions. It would be more logical to have a highly trained team of specialist staff that can provide support across the school in specific areas of additional intervention. For instance, a member of the support staff who has accessed an intensive training course in speech and language would be best deployed to deliver speech and language programmes across the school instead of delivering a wide range of non-specific interventions (for which no training has been accessed) in only one class. Another member of the support staff may have far greater experience with and the skills necessary to deliver numeracy interventions; yet another may be very effective in leading social skills intervention. It would appear short-sighted to limit such staff to delivering interventions in one class and more effective to ensure that they are deployed more widely across the school in their areas of specialism. To reinforce the importance of this practice I suggest that schools change the title for TAs or LSAs (Learning Support Assistants) and make reference to their enhanced training and expertise by calling them support specialists. Where I have observed this practice in schools there has been a very positive impact and many support staff have reported feeling more valued and respected by pupils and their parents.

It is prudent for any school to audit the skills of the support team on a regular basis and to determine where there are gaps in expertise so that training and development may be appropriately delivered. Such an audit will be informed by the evaluation of the impact of intervention, particularly where a number of similar interventions are being delivered by a range of personnel across the school and also by observations of delivery of interventions carried out by members of the SLT or the SENCO (see Chapter 7). In addition to this, the use of measureable targets on the Provision Map can help support TA performance management. It is my experience that the majority of support staff members welcome the opportunity to have quantifiable performance management pupil progress targets against which their performance may be measured.

Maintaining the Provision Map

Once finalised at the pupil progress review meeting, the draft Provision Map becomes a working document (Table 5.6). The teaching strategy box may be used by the teacher as

Table 5.6 Provision Map (draft)

Year 4	Date:		Term 4

Quality teaching strategies: visual timetable, task boards x 5, peer mentoring, grouping for support, cumulative reward system, writing frames, word banks, feelings wall, worry box, phone-a-friend, wobble seats x 3.

Interventions:

Intervention	Group size	Frequency/ duration/staff	Pupil	Entry data	Intervention target	Exit data	Outcome
Comprehension group	1:6	3 x 15 x 6 weeks HLTA	Amy Joe Dan Fred Bob Max	2c 2b 2c 2c 2b 2c	Plus one sub-level To use expression in reading To demonstrate understanding of text in conversation	2b 2a 2a 2a 2b	
Numeracy	1:6	4 x 20 x 6 weeks (early am) HLTA	Dan Fred Carl Amy Jane Sara	3c 3c 3b 3c 3c 3c	Plus one sub-level To be able to use multiplication facts (2, 5 and 10) confidently To use the 24-hour clock	3b 3b 3b 3c 3a 3a	
Paired reading	1:1	Daily, x 10, HLTA	Joe	2b	To re-engage with text Read with expression	2a	
Social skills	1:3	3 x 15		Leuven 1 2 4 2 3 2	To work on independent targets Organisational skills Working with others Working with others	Leuven 3 3 4 4 4 4	

(Social skills pupils: Carl, Jack, Wayne)

a reminder of strategies that have proved to be effective in this class or in other classes, recently or at other times. The teacher can refer to this section of the Provision Map when planning learning activities and when determining groupings, etc. It could also be used by members of the SLT when carrying out observations of teaching and learning to determine whether the teaching strategies discussed and advised on during a pupil progress review meeting are in place and fully embedded in daily classroom practice. For example, is a visual timetable in place and regularly referred to by pupils, thus indicating that it is part of normal classroom practice? The information in this box is also of significant importance to any supply teacher engaged to teach the class, as it provides evidence of the strategies pupils will expect to see in place and will support continuity and consistency if the regular teacher is absent.

Once the Provision Map has been agreed and staff identified to deliver each intervention, there should be an opportunity created in the timetable to ensure that the staff who will be delivering the interventions are fully prepared for them. The targets for each intervention need to be fully understood and any resources prepared. Time will need to be allocated in order to achieve this. Schools seem to be reluctant to take a break from the delivery of interventions even for a short period of time – the world will not end if there is no reading intervention for one or two days a term. I suggest that, following the drafting of the Provision Map, interventions (other than those that are part of a Statement) are suspended for a few days. This will allow support staff to prepare themselves and any equipment or resources necessary; to carry out any baseline assessment (though this should be minimal); and to familiarise themselves with the intervention targets as well as pupils who are new to them or to the intervention.

One of the keys to positive outcomes for intervention is effective communication between the person delivering the intervention and the class teacher. In this suggested model of specialist TAs delivering interventions across a school this can be problematic. Many TAs work part-time and most have additional duties at lunch and break times so it can be hard to find time to talk with the teacher. A simple solution is to develop a system for recording any relevant information and ensuring that the class teacher is quickly alerted to any issues identified by the TA. I recommend a basic pro-forma to record the pupils accessing the intervention, their attendance, the targets and any observations by the TA of issues relating to behaviour or progress that the teacher needs to be made aware of.

In the period following the pupil progress review meetings, when the majority of interventions are temporarily suspended, the TA can transfer the targets for the intervention from the Provision Map to the intervention target sheet and at this point an opportunity will be created for a dialogue about the targets between the TA and the class teacher (Tables 5.7 and 5.8). The linking of these targets to the TAs' performance management targets will reinforce their importance and the class teacher can be confident that the intervention will be appropriately focused. The intervention target sheet should be used as a regular communication tool. It is important to keep such systems of communication simple and the best practice I have observed has been just that: in one school all the intervention target sheets for each class are kept within a folder or file in the classroom. Every time a group leaves the class for an intervention the appropriate sheet goes with them. The TA uses the sheet to record absences so that any issues can be swiftly addressed and on each occasion will refer to the sheet and discuss the targets with the pupils, thereby ensuring that they are fully aware of what they are trying to achieve and are constantly reminded of why they are there and not in the classroom. Progress towards

Table 5.7 Intervention target sheet (blank)

Class:									Date commenced:		TA:		
Intervention:													
Timing, frequency and duration:													
Pupil names													
Dates													
Absence													
Targets	Observations and progress notes												

the targets is noted and shared with pupils who are consequently encouraged and motivated. Any issues regarding progress, behaviour or inappropriate placement in the group are recorded – not at length: short bullet points will suffice – and when the sheet is returned to the file in the classroom, if any comments have been added, the TA will place a post-it note on the outside of the folder or file so that the class teacher is alerted. This system is easy to set up and maintain, and the resulting documentation may be used by the class teacher when evaluating the impact of the interventions. For instance, if an intervention does not appear to have been successful for all pupils the question could be asked: were some of the least successful pupils frequently absent? It also ensures that where pupils are found to have been inappropriately placed in a group or intervention, swift action can be taken to address this.

It is not necessary to wait until the end of an intervention period to update a Provision Map. As the term progresses the teacher should update the Provision Map to show changes to teaching strategies where some have proved unsuccessful and others have been added, and to groups, frequency and timings of interventions as necessary. The best Provision Maps are those that are regularly scribbled on, adjusted and amended. If a pupil is experiencing a problem in a group, if the timetabling of a group is causing problems, if the frequency of the intervention sessions needs to be increased, adjustments should be made before the end of the intervention period and any changes recorded on the Provision Map.

The evaluated Provision Map

At the end of the intervention period the Provision Map needs to be evaluated. This will be achieved by entering the exit data for each intervention and then calculating the progress made by all pupils who have accessed each intervention. There may need to be reference made to the intervention target sheets and other datasets such as attendance and behaviour records (Table 5.9).

As this system may be composed of intervention and review intervals of different lengths I will explain how and when the Provision Map should be evaluated for each scenario.

If a school is both assessing and reviewing pupil progress six times per year, for the vast majority of interventions the end of the intervention period will coincide with the pupil progress review meetings and the exit data will always be current and relevant. However, for those schools assessing pupils six times per year but only reviewing progress four times per year, the end of the intervention period will not necessarily coincide with the pupil progress review meetings. This has been known to create a dilemma for some schools: when and how to enter the exit data for interventions on the Provision Map? For instance, in a school that assesses and reviews three times per year, an intervention that runs for six weeks will end before the end of the school's assessment interval. How should the outcome of the intervention be recorded in such an instance? As I have previously made clear, this system is intended to reduce bureaucracy and so I would advise against any additional assessment to measure progress in interventions and recommend that teachers still make use of the class-based assessments as the measure of impact, even though they may be carried out some time after the end of the intervention. After all, a true measure of impact is whether any progress gained through the provision of additional intervention is sustained.

Table 5.8 Intervention target sheet (completed)

Class 4				Date: Term 4			TA: Mrs C			

Intervention: Comprehension

Timing, frequency and duration: 3x15x6

Pupils: Amy, Joe, Dan, Fred, Bob, Max

Dates	10/4	12/4	13/4	18/4	20/4	21/4	25/4	27/4	28/4	5/5	7/5
Absence	Amy			Joe	Joe				Dan; Bob		

Targets plus one sub-level	Observation and progress notes
To use expression in reading	12/4 Joe very disruptive – lacks confidence
	13/4 Joe made some effort but easily distracted
To demonstrate understanding of text in conversation	20/4 Joe's absence has meant the group has made more progress over these two weeks
	21/4 Dan making good progress, read with real expression and understanding
	28/4 Dan and Bob in swimming gala, Joe very disruptive to the girls today

Table 5.9 Provision Map (evaluated)

Year 4	Date:	Term 4

Quality teaching strategies: visual timetable, task boards × 5, peer mentoring, grouping for support, cumulative reward system, writing frames, word banks, feelings wall, worry box, phone-a-friend, wobble seats × 3.

Interventions:

Intervention	Group size	Frequency/duration/staff	Pupil	Entry data	Intervention target	Exit data	Outcome
Comprehension group	1:6	3 × 15 × 6 weeks HLTA	Amy Joe Dan Fred Bob Max	2c 2b 2c 2c 2b 2c	Plus one sub-level To use expression in reading To demonstrate understanding of text in conversation	2b 2a 2a 2a 2b	Positive outcome for all except Joe – behaviour an issue.
Numeracy	1:6	4 × 20 × 6 weeks (early am) HLTA	Dan Fred Carl Amy Jane Sara	3c 3c 3b 3c 3c 3c	Plus one sub-level To be able to use multiplication facts (2, 5 and 10) confidently To use the 24-hour clock	3b 3b 3b 3c 3a 3a	4/6 plus one sub-level or more. Positive outcome. Amy attendance poor.
Paired reading	1:1	Daily, × 10, HLTA	Joe	2b	To re-engage with text Read with expression	2a	Good progress.
Social skills	1:3	3 × 15	Carl Jack Wayne	Leuven 1 2 4 2 3 2	To work on independent targets Organisational skills Working with others Working with others	Leuven 3 3 4 4 4 4	Leuven well-being and involvement improved.

An alternative to this system would be to use teacher assessment to record level of attainment at the point of cessation of intervention, measure progress over its duration and record this on the Provision Map in a divided exit data column (Table 5.10). At the next assessment point the teacher could enter the most up-to-date assessment intervention in the second half of the exit data column and thereby further analyse the impact of the intervention by demonstrating whether any initial gains have been sustained or built on.

Whatever the pattern of assessment and review, before each pupil progress review meeting, all exit data should be entered onto the Provision Map and the outcome of the intervention determined by the class teacher in preparation for that meeting. A copy of the evaluated Provision Map should be provided for the SLT and SENCO to consider in the week prior to the pupil progress review meeting. This will enable the school to build up a clear picture of 'what works' and so be able to disseminate that information to other teachers during the pupil progress review meetings and be best placed to consider alternatives to any unsuccessful interventions (see Chapter 4).

The teacher's review of the impact of interventions needs to be very rigorous in order to ensure that the intervention in place is effective enough. The Ofsted SEN review noted that 'even where assessment was accurate, timely, and identified the appropriate additional support, this did not guarantee that the support would be of good quality'. Further into the review it is reported that: 'Inspectors found that weaker providers did not always evaluate their own provision rigorously enough to identify whether what they were providing for individual pupils was sufficiently effective' (Ofsted 2010c, p. 40).

The evaluation of the impact of the intervention should be a calculation based on the difference between entry and exit data as well as an evaluation of whether the specific aspects of the target have been met. Particularly where there is no measurable difference in NC levels, progress against the specific targets should be recorded in the outcome column of the Provision Map. For instance, 'a pupil has moved from a low 3B to a high 3B' or 'a pupil has achieved the target of confidently using the 24hr clock'.

The evaluation of impact of intervention will be supported by a range of information other than hard assessment data. Pupil views (see Chapter 6) should be considered at this point: have any of the pupils commented that the behaviour of other pupils in the intervention group was a barrier to learning? Were there issues of timetabling or grouping? Information can also be gathered from the intervention target sheets: have there been a number of occasions when the intervention did not take place? The class teacher should also consider attendance and behaviour data and record any individual or group issues in the outcome column so that the evaluation of the intervention is complete.

Evaluated class Provision Maps may be used to support requests for external agency support or statutory assessment, as they can demonstrate how, despite significant intervention, an individual's progress over time has been inadequate, even though the same or similar interventions have had a positive effect on the progress of other pupils over the same period. In my experience this gives a more detailed and contextualised picture of the support a school has already provided when considering the need for statutory assessment than does a series of individual education plans (IEPs) that, where evaluated, often only record 'target not met'.

One of the key benefits of evaluative Provision Mapping is the information it provides to support school self-evaluation and development planning. This aspect will be explored further in Chapter 6.

Table 5.10 Provision Map (evaluated)

Year 4	Date:	Term 4

Quality teaching strategies: visual timetable, task boards × 5, peer mentoring, grouping for support, cumulative reward system, writing frames, word banks, feelings wall, worry box, phone-a-friend, wobble seats × 3.

Interventions:

Intervention	Group size	Frequency/ duration/staff	Pupil	Entry data	Intervention target	Exit data	Exit data 2	Outcome
Comprehension group	1:6	3 × 15 × 6 weeks HLTA	Amy Joe Dan Fred Bob Max	2c 2b 2c 2c 2b 2c	Plus one sub-level To use expression in reading To demonstrate understanding of text in conversation	2b 2b 2b 2b 2a 2b	2b 2a 2a 2c 2a 2b	Positive outcome for all except Joe – behaviour an issue. Review Fred.
Numeracy	1:6	4 × 20 × 6 weeks (early am) HLTA	Dan Fred Carl Amy Jane Sara	3c 3c 3b 3c 3c 3c	Plus one sub-level To be able to use multiplication facts (2, 5 and 10) confidently To use the 24-hour clock		3b 3b 3b 3c 3a 3a	4/6 plus one sub-level or more. Positive outcome. Amy attendance poor.
Paired reading	1:1	Daily, × 10, HLTA	Joe	2b	To re-engage with text Read with expression	2b	2a	Good progress.
Social skills	1:3	3 × 15	Carl Jack Wayne	Leuven 1 2 4 2 3 2	To work on independent targets Organisational skills Working with others Working with others	Leuven 3 3 4 3 3 2	Leuven 3 4 5 4 3 4	Leuven well-being and involvement improved.

What is the SENCO's role in Provision Mapping?

The SENCO's role in Provision Mapping is to:

• provide advice on interventions and strategies;
• evaluate the impact of interventions across the school;
• ensure that any training needs are met;
• ensure resources are adequate;
• discuss and agree prioritisation of provision with the SLT;
• ensure this information is shared with relevant bodies – governors, parents, LA, other schools, etc.

In this system it is the teacher who should be responsible both for the determination of the provision and the evaluation of it; the role of the SENCO is to advise on the most appropriate intervention and to support the teacher's evaluation by contributing additional evidence gathered from observations of the delivery of interventions. It is also the SENCO's responsibility to collate all the class Provision Maps following a pupil progress review period and to evaluate and record the impact of the interventions across the school to inform the school's self-evaluation and the governors (see Chapter 6). Any intervention that is proving to be less effective than it should, has been less effective in the past or is less effective in one class than in another should be investigated by the SENCO and action taken. Where intervention is new or where improvement is necessary, the SENCO should identify appropriate training and ensure that the relevant staff members access this and that impact is positive.

Although it may be the class teacher who selects an intervention, support with resourcing may be requested of the SENCO. It is usually the SENCO who holds the school's SEN budget and who can purchase additional resources. Through links with other schools, the SENCO may be able to source or borrow resources such as assessment materials, augmentation aids, etc.

A key action following pupil progress review meetings should be a discussion between the SENCO and the other members of the SLT to ensure that the team has accurately identified priorities for further development (for instance, that school-wide training on ASD needs to be provided) and is aware of their responsibility, both collectively and individually, in supporting the school to achieve those priorities.

It is definitely *not* the SENCO's role to write the Provision Map for teachers, and schools should beware of falling into this trap. In many schools, efficient and conscientious SENCOs have completed Provision Maps for teachers in the misguided belief that it is the completion of the Provision Map that is of paramount importance – it is not. The most important feature of this system is that it encourages the class teacher to assume greater responsibility and accountability for the progress of all pupils in the class, irrespective of any SEN. A perfectly completed Provision Map done *for* them and not *by* them will be counter-productive and will only reinforce their view that pupils who do not make adequate progress are 'someone else's problem'.

It is not the SENCO's job to send out Provision Maps to parents. The Provision Map is an excellent way of communicating with parents and should be shared with them, but it is class teachers who should do this, not SENCOs (See Chapter 6).

In every school the SENCO will be responsible for collating the evidence necessary to access external agencies such as physiotherapists, educational psychologists, etc., and for requests for statutory assessment. It will therefore be the SENCO who will be responsible for providing the evaluated class Provision Maps over a period of time to such agencies and it will also be the responsibility of the SENCO to provide data of provision made over time to support transition to another school. A tool that has proven popular with many SENCOs is a running record of intervention accessed (Table 5.11). I believe this can be easily compiled from class lists using the information from each class Provision Map. It may be added to over the course of a year to create a cumulative list of the different interventions accessed. This is not an evaluative exercise, merely a pupil-level record that serves to indicate the number and range of interventions which have been necessary to achieve the progress that has been made.

The interventions for the whole school are listed across the top of the table and the pupil names listed down the first column. The number of times an intervention is accessed across a year can be shown so that there is a clear indication of any need for long-term support in any one area. A copy of this record may be kept in each pupil's school file. If all other pupil names were removed, this record would be a useful document to support transition as an individualised record of the number of interventions accessed over time without trawling back through a number of Provision Maps. It would also be a way for the SENCO to quickly track whether any pupil has been accessing a worryingly high number of interventions. In this example the SENCO may well be most concerned about Mary Smith, but should be able to reconcile this hard data with the class Provision Map, the conversations in pupil progress review meetings, the observations of teaching in the class and in the interventions, and be confident that this high level of intervention is appropriate and necessary to ensure that progress is satisfactory. However, if the SENCO were concerned that this high level of intervention was having a negative impact upon Mary's progress or well-being, it would be a starting point for discussion with the class teacher and could indicate the need for a pupil case study to determine what her needs are and whether they are being met appropriately (see Chapter 7).

In my experience one of the benefits of adopting this Provision Mapping system is that, through greater accountability, teachers become more responsible for the outcomes of all pupils in their class. As they become more involved with monitoring and evaluating the impact of interventions and assume responsibility for the target-setting of interventions as well as in the classroom, the number of interventions they identify as necessary to secure good progress usually reduces. Generally, those teachers who have historically asked for a large number of interventions to support pupil progress in their class come to realise the importance of reducing the frequency and time a child spends accessing interventions that are not having sufficient impact upon progress. Where this does not happen SENCOs should play a part in challenging the number of interventions in place in any one class. Where there are a large number of interventions proposed by a teacher on the draft class Provision Map, the SENCO might work with the teacher to consider the order of priority of the interventions and the impact needed. There should be clear reasons given as to why an intervention is necessary and the teacher should be prepared to enter into a 'must, should, could' conversation:

- which interventions must happen;
- which should happen;
- which, in an ideal world, could happen.

Table 5.11 Intervention record sheet

Interventions Pupil	ELS	FLS	SALT	Physio	Maths	Toe/toe	Phonics	Social skills					
Joe Bloggs		X		X				X					
Mary Smith			XXX	XXX	XXX	XXX	XXX						
John Brown													
Amy Green					X		XXX	XXX					

Checklist for Provision Maps

- Are class Provision Maps drafted by class teachers?
- Do the Provision Maps show the key data including targets and entry and exit data?
- Are targets SMART?
- Can the Provision Map help teachers track pupil absence from the classroom?
- Are class Provision Maps evaluated by class teachers?
- Are evaluated Provision Maps used to support applications for external support or statutory assessment?
- Are intervention target sheets used to record key data for each intervention and as a simple system for sharing information between TA and teacher?
- Are interventions prioritised and is the number of interventions proposed reducing over time?

Chapter 6

Sharing information

Thus far I have demonstrated how Provision Mapping enables schools to track pupil progress and determine which provision to make and evaluate it. In this chapter I will show how it may be used to support self-evaluation and development planning, teachers' lesson planning, communication between staff, governors, other agencies and the 'structured conversation' with parents that has been shown to be such a powerful aspect of improving pupil outcomes in the Achievement for All Programme.

The need to improve parental confidence in a school's actions to meet the needs of pupils with SEN was highlighted in the findings of the Lamb Inquiry (2009), which, in turn, influenced many of the recommendations found in the Green Paper *Support and Aspiration: A New Approach to Special Educational Needs and Disability* (DfE 2011b). In this paper, the government pledged to reform education and health provision for pupils with special educational needs and to build parental confidence that schools are able to meet their child's needs (DfE 2011b). As part of the action identified to achieve this, the Achievement For All Programme, originally piloted between 2009 to 2011 in ten Local Authorities (460 schools) by the National Strategies, was rolled out nationally. Much like the system described in this book, there was little that was new in Achievement for All – it built on existing or previously recommended strategies and initiatives and linked together the assessment and monitoring of pupils, intervention and provision to meet need. However, it also involved parents in a prescribed way that had not been explored before.

The graphic in Figure 6.1 was used to demonstrate how the aspects of the Achievement for All Programme overlap and connect to make sure that the needs of children and young people can be met most effectively.

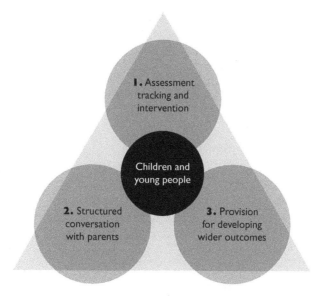

Figure 6.1 The principles of Achievement for All

Questions that will be answered in this chapter

- How do we share the draft Provision Map?
- How do we share the evaluated Provision Map?
- How do we gather and share pupil views?
- What are the confidentiality issues?

How do we share the draft Provision Map?

There are principally three groups of people with whom the class teacher needs to share the draft Provision Map:

- other staff and those people delivering the interventions;
- those pupils accessing the interventions;
- the parents of all pupils in the class.

Sharing information with other staff and those delivering the interventions

There may well be a need to share the class Provision Map with a range of other staff. For example, where pupils are accessing an intervention group drawn from more than one class, those teachers will need to be informed. Supply teachers, student teachers, temporary staff or volunteers will need to be made aware of the strategies in place to meet the needs of all pupils as well as the range of interventions being provided and their timetabling. Members of the SLT will need to use the Provision Map when carrying out observations of teaching to determine what impact the strategies listed on the Provision Map have on learning, behaviour, attendance, etc. For those people delivering the interventions there should be time set aside to enable them to prepare for the new period of intervention, and this time should include familiarisation with the Provision Map and in particular the intervention targets (see Chapter 5). They will need to be able to agree that aspects of intervention target-setting can be used to support their performance management targets and may necessitate further training and development (see Chapter 7).

Sharing information with pupils

While it is not necessary to share the Provision Map itself with pupils, if the targets for the intervention are shared regularly and frequently with them they will be better able to understand the reason for their absence from the classroom to access additional intervention and should be able to track their progress towards the targets, thus building confidence and self-esteem. This can be achieved through the use of intervention target sheets (see Chapter 5).

Sharing information with parents

It is critical for a school to share information with the parents of its most vulnerable pupils in such a way that they will easily understand the provision being made for their child and have confidence in those delivering it.

I suggest that the most appropriate way of sharing the Provision Map with parents is for the class teacher to anonymise the draft Provision Map and share it with parents during a parent consultation meeting (Table 6.1).

This ensures that all those involved see additional intervention as part of everyday classroom practice and reinforces the fact that it is the responsibility of the class teacher; it normalises intervention for parents and ensures they understand that any additional intervention will not be something completely separate and different from the learning their child will be engaged in in the classroom.

I believe it is important to share the Provision Map with *all* parents irrespective of whether or not their child is accessing additional intervention. This will help parents understand that at any point in their time at the school their child may need additional intervention, but that will not necessarily mean they will have SEN.

For those parents whose children are not currently having additional intervention the discussion could focus on the quality teaching strategies named on the Provision Map and how those strategies might be supporting all pupils. The presence of entry levels on the draft Provision Map will enable the class teacher to explain to these parents how pupils are identified for additional intervention and why their child does not need to access any at this particular time.

For parents of pupils who are identified for intervention, the Provision Map can be very reassuring. They can understand how the intervention groups are composed and why their child needs to access them. They can also see how often and for how long the intervention will be delivered. If the intervention is to be delivered before or after school there can be a conversation about the need for punctuality or any clashes with out-of-school activities. Through discussion about the intervention targets parents can be helped to understand how to support their child at home and what they should expect to see in terms of progress if the intervention has been successful. Parents of pupils who have had

Table 6.1 Parent Provision Map

Year 4   Date: Term 4

Quality teaching strategies: visual timetable, task boards × 5, peer mentoring, grouping for support, cumulative reward system, writing frames, word banks, feelings wall, worry box, phone-a-friend, wobble seats × 3.

Interventions:

Intervention	Group size	Frequency/ duration/staff	Pupil	Entry data	Intervention target	Exit data	Outcome
Comprehension group	1:6	3 × 15 × 6 weeks HLTA		2c 2b 2c 2c 2b 2c	Plus one sub-level To use expression in reading To demonstrate understanding of text in conversation		
Numeracy	1:6	4 × 20 × 6 weeks (early am) HLTA		3c 3c 3b 3c 3c 3c	Plus one sub-level To be able to use multiplication facts (2, 5 and 10) confidently To use the 24-hour clock		
Paired reading	1:1	Daily, × 10, HLTA		2b	To re-engage with text Read with expression		
Social skills	1:3	3 × 15		Leuven 1 2 4 2 3 2	To work on independent Organisational skills Working with others Working with others		

intervention which has now ceased can be reassured that it has ceased because the target has been reached and parents can remain confident that rigorous monitoring of their child's progress will be ongoing.

I suggest that in the parent consultation meeting teachers have an anonymised copy of the draft Provision Map to hand together with a highlighter pen. When talking with the parents of a child accessing an intervention the teacher can highlight the intervention on the Provision Map, explain what level the child is currently working at and which level they will be working at once they have attained the intervention target. The target grade could be written into the blank exit data column so that parents are aware of the level they should anticipate their child will be working at when attainment is next reported back to them. The class teachers can discuss the intervention targets themselves, reassuring parents that the targets are linked to those in the classroom. When explaining how the parents can help with supporting the achievement of these targets at home it may be sensible to make a note of these ideas in the blank outcome column on the Provision Map. The parents can take this away with them for reference until their next discussion with the teacher.

In all the work I have done with parents, they have always indicated that they appreciate this contextual evidence far more than they do an IEP. The targets are SMART and they make sense; the parents can tell what intervention is provided for the whole class; some will be reassured that their child is only accessing one intervention while others will be equally reassured if their child is accessing many. They know that the system in place in the school means that their child cannot 'fall through the net' and they also understand that their child does not need to be given a potentially limiting, deficit label (SEN) in order to access extra provision.

How do we share the evaluated Provision Map?

The evaluated Provision Map contains evidence of the impact of the interventions over the previous period of intervention. This information should have been shared by the class teacher with the SENCO and SLT before the pupil progress review meeting, but it needs to be reflected upon further to support the school's strategic prioritisation of resources and staff. The effectiveness of each intervention must be considered and this information should be used to help the class teacher determine:

- whether to continue or discontinue it;
- whether it should be extended to make provision for more or larger groups of pupils;
- whether it should be delivered in a different way;
- whether it should be delivered over a different length of time or at a different time of day.

It should be used by the SENCO to determine:

- whether there are any staff training needs that should be met to secure the greater success of a programme.

Conversely, where an intervention has been extremely successful, the SENCO should consider:

- whether it can be used more widely throughout the school;
- whether it could be shared with other schools in the locality.

Table 6.2 Evaluation of impact of interventions

Evaluation of impact of interventions																	Date: September–December 2011
% making accelerated progress/ reaching targets	Speech link	Language link	BEAM	1:1 reading	ELS	Literacy support group 1 & 2	Writing support	Phonics group	Reading reflex	Lit. booster	Comprehension group	Numeracy group	Springboard	Extension maths	Number booster	Lego therapy	Therapeutic play
Year R	80	80															
Class 1			25	75	75			76									
Class 2			80	75	80		0	71	80	0							100
KS 1	80	80	52	75	77		0	73	80	0							100
Class 3			100	80		66	33	0	100	100							100
Class 4			100			80	80		50	100			66				
				75		75	100			100							
Class 5										33	pos		100	66	75	75	66
Class 6				100						0	50		100	25	66	80	
KS2			100	85	77	74	71	0	75	67	50		88	45	70	85	66
School average	80	80	76	82	77	74	53	49	77	55	50		88	45	70	85	83

Sharing information with governors, Ofsted, etc.

If all of the class Provision Maps are collated and the impact of provision across the school is evaluated by the SENCO this information can be used to support the school's self-evaluation and reported to governing bodies and to Ofsted (Table 6.2).

The evaluation of impact of interventions across the school is vital. It allows the school to determine where there are areas for development and any identified training and development needs that can be added to the school development plan and budgeted for, along with the purchase of any resources needed to support the efficient delivery of the interventions. It helps the school to swiftly and appropriately bring about change to pupil support and ensure that 'value for money' is being achieved. Value for money is not a quantitative judgement; instead it is a measure of whether accelerated progress has been achieved in the time allocated for the intervention. If pupils who access it make more progress over the course of the intervention than their peers who do not then the intervention has had an impact that would reflect value for money irrespective of the financial cost. This information is of particular relevance to governing bodies, and I suggest that following each period of assessment and review, the impact of the interventions should be shared with the governing body to help it consider the effectiveness of the school in improving outcomes for the most vulnerable pupils (see Tables 6.2 and 6.3).

Ofsted judges schools on the impact of the interventions to support pupil progress, and in its current subsidiary guidance to inspectors it advises them to 'note if pupils who receive additional interventions are demonstrating accelerated or sustained progress indicating that the interventions may be effective'(Ofsted 2012, p. 9). It is expected that schools' self-evaluation will contain evidence of the impact of intervention and this will form part of the information gathering for Ofsted inspectors. From September 2012 when inspections will be carried out with minimal notice, schools will be expected to provide evidence of self-evaluation to inspectors as they commence their inspection. The information will therefore need to be provided in a succinct and easy-to-interpret format. I suggest that such a table demonstrating the impact of interventions over a term or a year would be particularly valuable and would enable inspectors to swiftly identify strengths and weaknesses that could determine or discount an inspection trail. The evaluated Provision Maps would provide further detail and would support schools in providing the pupil case studies that are usually requested by inspectors (see Chapter 7). If the school were to summarise the evaluation of impact of interventions and prepare a statement for the school self-evaluation document it would take the form as shown in Table 6.3.

Sharing information with outside agencies

An evaluated Provision Map can support requests for additional support from outside agencies, as it can demonstrate that a range of approaches and intervention have been provided and what impact they have had. It can demonstrate, for example, that an intervention that has been highly successful for most pupils has not had the same impact on the identified pupil; that an alternative intervention was attempted but that this too failed to secure the accelerated progress achieved by other pupils, and that therefore there needs to be further assessment or investigation of the needs of this pupil and possibly a statutory assessment. Because all the targets are SMART, the progress towards them will be relevant. Targets from external agencies such as speech and language therapists or physiotherapists can be entered onto and evaluated on the Provision Map for individuals. This action will

Table 6.3 Text version of impact of interventions

Literacy interventions in KS1 result in 51% of pupils attending making accelerated progress and/or attaining targets.

Literacy interventions in KS2 result in 60% of pupils making accelerated progress and/or attaining targets.

Action (training) is being taken to develop skills and expertise of those delivering interventions in KS1 and KS2 where progress is less than good – supported through performance management targets and mentoring.

Maths interventions in KS1 are delivered in class; 89% of pupils are on track to achieve age related levels at end of KS2.

Maths interventions in KS2 result in 68% of pupils making accelerated progress and/or attaining target. There is a notable gender imbalance – boys outperform girls in interventions.

Social skills interventions have resulted in a reduction in the number of recorded behaviour incidents; however, the introduction of peer mediation in term 2 may also have affected this. There have been no exclusions this year. C&I pupils make good progress overall.

Speech and language interventions are in place and pupils identified through Speechlink and Language link make good progress through programmes of support. Speech and language therapist not available.

BEAM is under review – the impact of this intervention although measured in targets achieved is hard to detect or measure in class, and the SENCO is investigating the possibility of delivering training on BEAM and Clever Fingers to CTs in order to ensure that the strategies that are in use in classes meet the needs of these pupils without the need for out-of-class support.

mean that the class teacher has a better understanding of the needs of those pupils and how best to meet them.

Despite this, some pupils may still need an IEP or a PSP (pastoral support plan) or BP (behaviour plan). However, in such cases, because the school is only using these plans with a small number of pupils, these pupils stand out and become more high profile than they would have done as one of the 50 or so pupils with IEPs that was common in many primary schools in the past.

How should we gather and share pupils' views?

One of the most critical features of successful intervention is that the pupils engage with this additional provision. If a pupil is reluctant to attend, or cannot see the point of accessing intervention that takes him or her away from the classroom, then the success of the intervention may well be limited. Class teachers need to gather pupil views on the additional intervention and add this information to their evaluation of the outcome of the provision. This does not need to be in a formalised, quantitative way; for example, it is not necessary to use questionnaires or surveys. The views of pupils should be collected principally through conversation and observation. Most class teachers are well aware of pupils who are hesitant about leaving the classroom to attend an intervention – the pulling of faces, the dejected appearance, the reluctance to leave; and most are aware of those who cannot wait to leave the class for an intervention; eager excitement and obvious enthusiasm. But often there needs to be a further examination of these responses. The class teacher will want to know whether the grouping is working for the pupil; the only girl in a group of boys might be struggling; the mix of Year 5 girls in an intervention that takes place after a playtime could be affected by social issues that may have arisen during the break. The timetabling issues also need unpicking; is the child missing a favourite lesson or an area of the curriculum in which they excel, to go to an intervention group that is a continuation of the very thing he or she has struggled with for half of the morning?

These 'soft' data are critical when it comes to assessing the impact of the intervention and when planning for further intervention. I would suggest that at some point during the intervention period, and not just at the very end, the views of pupils are sought and recorded on the intervention target sheet. The person most suited to conducting this conversation will vary – it could be the class teacher, it could be the person delivering the intervention or another member of the school staff. The information could also be augmented by comments from parents or other pupils. The information collected in this way should be used by class teachers to contribute to their evaluation of the impact of any intervention, and any specific issues raised during the pupil progress review meeting so that appropriate action can be considered by the class teacher in consultation with the SLT members and SENCO.

What are the confidentiality issues?

As you will see in Table 6.1, the draft Provision Map has had all names removed. Some schools question whether this level of anonymisation is sufficient and worry that parents could still attribute levels to individual children. In group interventions I doubt that this would be true, unless all pupils were working at the same level, but I do acknowledge that for pupils accessing one-to-one interventions it could be difficult to retain confidentiality. For instance, a pupil accessing counselling or anger management might be easily identified by other parents from the anonymised Provision Map and this should be avoided. Table 6.4 gives an example of how the draft Provision Map can be further anonymised to ensure that these pupils cannot be identified. Provision Maps submitted to support applications for statutory assessment or circulated to outside agencies should be fully anonymised.

Checklist for sharing information

- Do teachers share anonymised versions of the Provision Map with all parents at parent consultation meetings?
- Do parents understand the interventions in place for their child and how they can support their child?
- Are Provision Maps shared with support staff, temporary staff, volunteers, etc.?
- Are evaluated Provision Maps used to calculate the impact of interventions across the school?
- Is this shared with governors and incorporated into the school's self-evaluation in an easy-to-read format?
- Are Provision Maps used to support requests for support or statutory assessment?
- Are pupil views collected and acted upon?
- Even though we share the Provision Map, do we maintain confidentiality?

Table 6.4 Parent Provision Map 2

Year 4	Date:	Term 4

Quality teaching strategies: visual timetable, task boards × 5, peer mentoring, grouping for support, cumulative reward system, writing frames, word banks, feelings wall, worry box, phone-a-friend, wobble seats × 3.

Interventions:

Intervention	Group size	Frequency/ duration/staff	Pupil	Entry data	Intervention target	Exit data	Outcome
Comprehension group	1:6	3 × 15 × 6 weeks HLTA		2c 2b 2c 2c 2b 2c	Plus one sub-level To use expression in reading To demonstrate understanding of text in conversation		
Numeracy	1:6	4 × 20 × 6 weeks (early am) HLTA		3c 3c 3b 3c 3c 3c	Plus one sub-level To be able to use multiplication facts (2, 5 and 10) confidently To use the 24-hour clock		
Social skills	1:3	3 × 15		Leuven 1 2 4 2 3 2	To work on independent Organisational skills Working with others Working with others		

Chapter 7

Development

The explicit message in Ofsted's 2010 SEN review was that the difference to pupil outcomes is made by good teaching in the classroom. All pupils have a right to experience good or better teaching but there is always room for improvement, and schools have a responsibility to ensure that teachers have the necessary skills and knowledge to meet the needs of all pupils, but particularly those pupils who are vulnerable to experiencing barriers to participation and engagement with learning. No matter how effective additional interventions are, they will not make up for inadequate or satisfactory teaching. And no matter how good classroom teaching is, some children will always need additional, high-quality support or intervention.

In the SEN review Ofsted noted that in schools where:

> support staff had enough knowledge and understanding to meet the needs of the majority of pupils as a matter of course . . . [these schools] . . . had fewer pupils who required additional intervention. There was therefore more time for specialist staff to assist teachers and help meet the needs of pupils with more complex difficulties from a base of very good teaching and learning. These schools usually had a rolling programme of learning and development.
>
> (Ofsted 2010c, p. 48)

This chapter is concerned with how to ensure that there is a base of very good teaching and learning in your school and a rolling programme of learning and development that leads to improved pupil outcomes. In a successful school, self-review and self-challenge will be integral to the school's practice and lead to action that secures improvement. This Provision Mapping system will guarantee that your staff will adopt a more reflective approach to teaching and that practice will constantly change and improve through opportunities for training and development.

Questions that will be answered in this chapter

- How do we identify that teaching or intervention needs to improve?
- How do we bring about improvement?
- How do we ensure that improvement is sustained?

How do we identify that teaching or intervention needs to improve?

The key to early identification of inadequate practice lies in the analysis of progress and the evaluation of impact of interventions described in previous chapters. However, the triangulation of the evidence from data analysis along with that from observation of teaching and work scrutiny is essential. Links must be made between these evidence bases so that accurate evaluation of the quality of teaching can be made and early identification of interventions that are failing to have the desired impact addressed.

In one school the mid-year (Term 3) analysis of data of a Year 3 Class showed that a significant proportion of the pupils had failed to make one sub-level of progress and were therefore considered to be 'not on track'. However, observations of teaching in this class had been judged outstanding on the past three occasions. The evidence gathered from work scrutiny showed that pupils were achieving learning objectives, guidance to pupils was clear about how and what to do to make progress and the SLT felt confident that all elements of good/outstanding teaching were in place to enable progress to be achieved. The class teacher was very demoralised by the apparent lack of progress until the SLT asked him to reflect on the APP (assessing pupil progress) evidence. From this more detailed analysis he could show that all those pupils who had not made a sub-level progress had started the year within the sub-level at a low level and were now at least secure, and most were at high level. The SLT was confident that progress was being made, that pupils were being well taught and that there was still a strong probability that these pupils could reach their targets by the end of the year. Although the close tracking of progress was enabling the SLT to ask challenging questions of teachers, the consideration of other evidence was crucial to the evaluation.

However, in the same school the teacher of the parallel Year 3 class showed similar mid-year data (a high proportion of pupils not on track for end-of-year targets). The most recent observation of teaching in this class had been satisfactory and the most recent work scrutiny revealed a lack of evidence that the teacher was marking work with clear guidance to the pupils on how to improve their work. By linking all this evidence together the SLT identified concerns and took action in line with the school's teaching and learning policy; the teacher was immediately provided with support and opportunities for development, a mentor was put in place, and developmental targets were set with repeat observation of teaching timetabled for four weeks hence.

Review of the impact of interventions should include data gathered from observation of delivery of interventions by support staff. This type of observation is often neglected and should be more highly prioritised in schools. A cycle of observations should be planned and published to support staff in the same way as the cycle for planned observations is published for teachers. Support staff should become familiar with being observed and should be encouraged to view this as a developmental opportunity. The observations should also be linked into the performance management targets for each member of staff. With the greater emphasis Ofsted is placing on the delivery of interventions, in particular to improve reading, it is usual practice for Ofsted inspectors to observe some sessions of intervention during an inspection. Schools that use the system of Provision Mapping described in this book and who regularly observe the delivery of interventions will be able to demonstrate that they have an evaluation of the impact of interventions that goes beyond a data exercise and incorporates the views of pupils and the outcome of observations.

Another way of establishing whether teaching and/or intervention is having a sufficient impact on pupil progress is to carry out a pupil case study (Table 7.1). This approach is currently favoured by Ofsted although at the time of writing it is unclear whether Ofsted inspections from September 2012 will continue to examine case studies produced by schools. However, it is still a useful tool for schools to provide as supporting evidence. Schools have generally been asked to provide three case studies during an inspection, showing the impact of intervention on pupils from a range of vulnerable groups. This proforma is helpful; its use will ensure that all aspects have been considered and any issues identified as a result of this action should be addressed.

When carrying out a case study, I suggest that schools, having identified their most vulnerable groups, select one pupil as representative of each group and class teachers complete one each, retrieving the evidence needed to complete the case study. The completion of the case study by class teachers will reveal whether there are any barriers to staff obtaining information about a pupil in their care, whether they know the pupils well and whether they have a sound knowledge of their pupils' current progress and the impact of any intervention to improve it.

How do we bring about improvement?

It is important to mention here the critical aspects of good classroom teaching:

- sound understanding of the levels pupils are working at and next steps for development;
- good differentiation (that is, teaching that is appropriately directed and not just the 'watering down' of a task);
- good understanding of strategies that would successfully support pupils who are vulnerable to underachievement and those strategies needed to support the high-frequency need types (ASD, ADHD, dyslexia, speech and language, etc.);
- planned and effective use of additional staff, ICT and resources;
- lessons that are challenging and well paced with frequent checks of understanding.

How to achieve this teaching across the school should be the single most important issue facing any school's SLT.

Good teachers can find it difficult to 'blow their own trumpets'; they often prefer to share what hasn't worked rather than what has, and schools seldom structure opportunities for sharing good practice into their plan for CPD. I suggest schools timetable opportunities for sharing good practice into the annual calendar and ensure that all members of staff contribute to this activity. Many staff will have a wealth of experience

Table 7.1a Pupil case study

Pupil case study	English	Maths	Science
Pupil:			
Year/class:			
Vulnerable group (including SEN level and dimension)			
Pen picture			
Prior attainment data. Previous KS levels			
Current NC levels			
End-of-year targets			
End of Key Stage (FFTD) targets			
On track?			
Attendance			
Behaviour/exclusion history			
Bullying incidents			
Current provision and impact (evidenced on Provision Map and/or IEP)			
External agency involvement			
Pupil views			
Parent views			
Comments			

Table 7.1b Pupil case study

Where evidence can be found	How the case study will be completed
• Attendance sheets/attendance figures in SIMS • Prior attainment, current NC levels in SIMS and inter-year progress tracking sheets • Reports from other agencies • Medical diagnosis • Time line of intervention • Provision Maps/IEP/PSP (inc. outcomes) • Target review sheets • Records – parent meetings • Pupil views • Parent views • Pupil timetable • In-class observations • Pupil shadowing • Evidence that school is seeking, acting on and evaluating external agency involvement • Risk assessment • Work scrutiny • Tracking of well-being and involvement	• Identify vulnerable groups • Identify one pupil from each vulnerable group • Complete case study form • Shadow (unannounced) • Check all information is easily accessible, up to date and dated • Does provision match need? • Scrutinise timetable – % absence from classroom • Overview of support – who is providing the majority of the support? • Is progress accelerating? • Can the CT/form tutor produce this data? • Interview pupil

and have developed a range of effective strategies over the years, while others will have new ideas they have recently tried out or ideas picked up from training. The sharing of these ideas is essential and can be achieved during a professional development meeting. These meetings could be held three times per year and during the meeting staff can share good practice and decide which strategies they will use with their own class. I suggest that the quality teaching box on the Provision Map be updated at this meeting (Table 7.2). Getting the staff to complete this task during the meeting will ensure that all staff members do so. Don't let staff put it off until later when it will most likely be overlooked but instead ensure that staff members spend some time together focusing on what will work in the classroom, and record their ideas in the appropriate section of their class Provision Map.

All the quality teaching boxes for each class should look somewhat different. No class is the same as any other; some will have a predominance of one need type and teachers will employ more strategies to meet those needs than to meet other needs. Schools may find it helpful to compose a generic list of the strategies that are known to be effective and teachers could use that list to inform their choice about strategies for their own class, but this section of the Provision Map should be personalised to the class. The SLTs should be able to use that section of the Provision Map to see what the predominant need type in the class is and how it is being supported. They should also be able to use it when carrying out a classroom observation to enable them to observe the strategies embedded in classroom practice. This link to classroom observation will ensure there is a constant focus on meeting the needs of those who are most vulnerable to experiencing exclusionary barriers to learning, whether they have SEN or not.

The example included contains a high number of strategies to meet the needs of pupils exhibiting high anxiety (worry box, phone-a-friend, feelings wall), a need for social modelling (peer mentoring, grouping for support) and a need for organisational structure (visual timetable, task boards). It would appear that a high proportion of the pupils in this class may be exhibiting ASD traits and some may also have ADHD tendencies (wobble seats).

If staff are to make the best use of the Provision Map as a method of evaluating the impact of intervention and changing practice as a result, then this box on the Provision Map should be the most regularly adjusted and changed. It should be used as an *aide-mémoire* by teachers when planning. A good sign that a Provision Map is being properly used is that it is scribbled on, grubby or coffee stained! If used properly, as strategies become less effective they will be crossed out and new ones added. For instance, a class such as the one in the example, that starts the year with high levels of anxiety and needing significant support in this area may well see the need for such support reduce as the impact of the strategies takes hold. In such instances the quality teaching box of the Provision Map should be adjusted when the changes are made – it is not necessary to wait for the next pupil progress review meeting to do this. As the Provision Map is brought to the pupil progress review meeting, the extensive discussion in that meeting about how to improve the classroom or quality first teaching should be reflected in the strategies listed in the quality teaching box which could be added to or amended at the meeting.

Any identified gaps in the training, skills or knowledge of class teachers in meeting the needs of vulnerable pupils must be addressed with urgency. A starting point could be the materials that compose the National Strategies Inclusion Development Programme (DCSF 2007). The 2010 Ofsted review of SEN stated that effective schools:

Table 7.2 Provision Map with Wave 1

Year 4		Date:		Term 4			
Quality teaching strategies: visual timetable, task boards x 5, peer mentoring, grouping for support, cumulative reward system, writing frames, word banks, feelings wall, worry box, phone-a-friend, wobble seats x 3.							

Interventions:

Intervention	Group size	Frequency/ duration/staff	Pupil	Entry data	Intervention target	Exit data	Outcome

[U]sually had a rolling programme of learning and development for all staff that included extending the teaching strategies that had been found to be successful, particularly for children and young people with special educational needs. The main aim of the National Strategies' Inclusion Development Programme was to improve 'quality first teaching'.[1] In a few of the schools visited, this resource had been used to improve the knowledge and understanding of all staff.

(Ofsted 2010c, p. 48)

The Inclusion Development Programme audit tools can be used by schools to determine gaps in knowledge and identify training needs. The training can be delivered at a whole-school level or it can be tailored to meet the needs of a group or an individual. It would be important to extend the training to support staff members who will need to be made aware of the most commonly effective strategies when trying to meet the needs of pupils with SEN. Although archived by the current government they remain a powerful aid to staff SEN development.

In addition to these archived materials the government has provided advanced training materials for teachers of pupils with SEN (http://www.education.gov.uk/lamb/) which cover the main need types.

All identified training needs should be recorded in the school's self-evaluation and the cost of the training and how its impact will be measured included in the school's improvement plan.

How do we ensure that improvement is sustained?

Through use of this system, ensuring the regular and frequent review of pupil progress and triangulating this information with teaching observations and work scrutiny, a school can guarantee that a focus on the quality of teaching is sustained. If this system is linked into the performance management cycle the focus will be ongoing and developmental.

Performance management

Whatever action is identified to address performance should be linked to the school's performance management process. The DfE has published new guidance on teacher performance management. From September 2012 schools will be able to create their own policy and the requirement to adhere to a strict timetable for performance management is removed. In light of this it would be sensible for schools to align the performance management cycle with the pupil progress review cycle to ensure that performance management pupil progress targets are set and reviewed in relation to the most recent and relevant pupil progress data. It would therefore be appropriate to arrange the target setting meetings for a week or so after the first stage in the assessment and review cycle. The performance management of support staff should also be aligned to this cycle as the setting of measurable intervention targets should enable the pupil progress targets for support staff to be clearly defined. In addition to the pupil progress targets, professional development targets can also be linked to pupil progress review. Where whole-school or individual training needs are identified as a result of data analysis and pupil progress review, targets should be set and training accessed to ensure a successful outcome.

All schools should be evaluating the impact of training on the performance of their staff and should be able to share this information with governors. As schools find it increasingly difficult to release staff to attend training, from both a cover and a cost point of view, it becomes increasingly more important to get 'value for money' from all training. Schools should have an established practice of evaluation and dissemination or feedback to other staff following each attendance at training, and should be able to evidence the impact of training on teaching and outcomes. For instance, a school that identifies the teaching of maths as an area for development and sends a teacher to be trained as a Numbers Count teacher will want to:

- evaluate the impact of this very expensive training;
- ensure that the skills and knowledge gained by the trainee are disseminated as widely as possible;
- ensure that there is a discernible impact on teaching and that this is reflected in pupil progress and outcomes.

Checklist for development

1 Do we triangulate information from pupil progress data analysis, observation and work scrutiny to determine any areas for development?
2 Do we have timetabled opportunities for staff to share good practice and update their Provision Map three times per year?
3 Are we using the IDP materials to enhance staff understanding of effective ways of meeting the most commonly occurring special educational needs?
4 Do we observe the delivery of interventions and through this identify any training and development needs among support staff?
5 Are our support staff being set appropriate pupil progress targets as part of their performance management?
6 Do we have a performance management cycle that is linked to the pupil progress review cycle and is thus able to influence the setting and review of targets?
7 Do we get good value for money from training? Does our school evaluate and disseminate training to other staff, enter it into the school's self-evaluation and share that evaluation with governors?

Note

1 http://webarchive.nationalarchives.gov.uk/20110202093118/http:/nationalstrategies. standards.dcsf.gov.uk/search/inclusion/results/nav:46335

Chapter 8

How to put evaluative Provision Mapping in place in your school

The system described in this book is tried and tested. It is based on several years of development with primary schools in Kent where teachers and headteachers report that they have found it to be sensible, manageable and effective in improving outcomes. It places the class teacher at the heart of everything schools do to ensure that pupils make the best progress possible, and it enhances information sharing with parents, governors and the LA. It ensures that schools know the effectiveness of any action that is taken; whether it is successful in improving outcomes and how effective any training is in improving the quality of teaching. This chapter is concerned with how to successfully establish this system in your school.

You may have some or all of the elements of this system already and will only need to consider and slightly adapt your practice to align it with the principles of this system and ensure that you are getting the maximum impact from all that you do. Alternatively you may have to start afresh; to establish regular assessment, analysis and review cycles; and you may have to introduce Provision Maps to your school staff members, governors, and to the parents of your pupils. Governors may never have had a role in challenging the impact of the interventions you provide and may need support and guidance to make that level of challenge appropriately. Teachers may need intensive support with understanding their responsibility for pupil progress in interventions and their role in Provision Mapping. SENCOs may need support in how to evaluate the impact of the interventions in place across your school.

The importance of the headteacher's role

Once established, the system should run through the course of a year with little need for adjustment, but there are some factors that would limit the effectiveness of this system. In only two schools with which I have worked has this system not been effective and in both of those schools the system was not well led by the headteacher. As it is dependent upon links to the performance management cycle, the governor meeting cycle and the whole school timetable, it must be strongly led to ensure that all stages of the system are effective. Staff members must be helped to adhere to the sometimes challenging demands of the timescale and to become proficient at data analysis and target-setting, but they must also be held to account if they do not. This can be achieved through the performance management system but would need the active involvement of the headteacher to ensure it has the necessary impact. Governors need support and direction to enable them to ask the right questions and to seek information of the highest quality, and will rely on the headteacher for this. Parents will need to be informed and those who have had long experience of using IEPs will need careful support to understand the change to Provision Mapping. This level of communication will be improved by the headteacher's involvement. Self-evaluation and school development planning, led by the headteacher, will be enhanced by this system as will any conversation about progress, attainment and intervention with Ofsted during inspection. For any school to be fully effective all classroom teaching must be at least good; where it is less than good this system will support a headteacher in securing rapid and sustainable improvement in the quality of teaching across the school.

The school calendar

The first action that I recommend schools take in introducing this system to their school is to establish a school calendar at the start of the year with all aspects of this system clearly laid out (Table 8.1).

This calendar has been created for a school that intends to assess and review six times per year, but if you were to choose to assess and/or review less frequently you would need to adjust the calendar accordingly. It is linked to the proposed three-year cycle for moderation, the performance management cycle, parent consultation and governing body meetings. Once the annual calendar has been agreed it should be published to all staff members, so that they are fully prepared for every stage of the system and can plan their activities accordingly. If they are made fully aware of critical dates in advance, teachers should not plan to be absent from school, for instance, for class trips, during assessment or review week. It should be published to governors so that they can arrange their formal and informal visits, the headteacher performance management target-setting and review meetings, and their governing body meeting cycle. These can then be aligned with times when the school will be able to provide it with the most up-to-date information on the percentage of pupils on track to achieve their targets, the progress being made by vulnerable groups and the impact of the most recently delivered interventions.

Once the timetable has been published the SLT should consider each of the aspects of the system and review whether there needs to be any change to practice. I have included aids for self-review for each aspect of the system and would encourage a school SLT to spend time honestly reflecting on the questions and making notes of any areas where change or development is necessary. The following pages include examples of tools to support school self-evaluation of its practice in:

- assessment (Table 8.2)
- data entry and analysis (Table 8.3)
- pupil progress review (Table 8.4)
- Provision Mapping (Table 8.5)
- sharing information (Table 8.6)
- training and development (Table 8.7).

Table 8.1 Annual school Provision Mapping calendar

2011/12	Term 1	Term 2	Term 3	Term 4	Term 5	Term 6
Week 1	Baseline assessment if necessary	Parent consultation	Moderation P Scales	Parent consultation and questionnaire		
Week 2		Performance management target-setting	Professional development meeting	Performance management review meeting Pupil questionnaire		Moderation history
Week 3	Professional development meeting	Moderation speaking and listening	Observations	Govenors' meeting	Moderation maths	Professional development meeting
Week 4	Moderation reading	Governors' meeting	Moderation writing	Moderation science	Observations	Performance management review meeting
Week 5	Observations		Assessment Data analysis Pupil views	Assessment Data analysis Pupil views		Assessment Data analysis Pupil views
Week 6			Review Draft Provision Map	Review Draft Provision Map	Assessment Data analysis Pupil views	Review (transition) Draft Provision Map Report to parents Gov meeting
Week 7	Assessment Data analysis Pupil views	Assessment Data analysis Pupil views			Review Draft Provision Map	
Week 8	Review Draft Provision Map	Review Draft Provision Map				

Table 8.2 Assessment

Assessment	Yes	No	Needs developing
Are we using reliable assessment that tells us what we need to know?			
If we use tests, are they measuring what we have taught?			
If we use teacher assessment, is it moderated regularly and are all our teachers levelling appropriately?			
Do we assess often enough and at roughly equal intervals?			
Do we baseline on entry if necessary?			
Do we use relevant assessment tools to measure impact of non-academic intervention?			
Do we use our assessments to plan for future learning, including in interventions?			

Table 8.3 Data entry and analysis

Data entry and analysis	Yes	No	Needs developing
Are class teachers entering and analysing class-level assessment data?			
Do class teachers use a RAG rating system consistently to highlight any inadequate progress?			
Are class teachers using this analysis of data to prompt rigorous self-review?			
Is the SLT making appropriate and useful school level analyses of progress; in particular the progress of vulnerable groups?			
Are links being made between different datasets; records of observation, pupil views, attendance and behaviour?			
Are all staff members aware of who the most vulnerable groups in the school are?			
Is the school setting challenging enough targets?			

Table 8.4 Pupil progress review

Pupil progress review	Yes	No	Needs developing
Are the meetings timetabled to take place immediately following in-class assessment?			
Are the class teachers following the school's policy on preparation for these meetings? Has the SLT been provided with class-level data analyses and corresponding evaluated class Provision Maps prior to the meeting?			
Is the SLT fully prepared for each meeting?			
Do the meetings focus on improving whole class teaching?			
Does the SENCO attend each of the meetings?			
Is the evaluated class Provision Map discussed and does the school have a clear picture of 'what works'?			
As an outcome of the meeting does each class have a new Provision Map listing effective teaching strategies and details of additional intervention?			
Are links made between the outcome of the meetings and performance management, self-evaluation and school development planning?			

Table 8.5 Provision Mapping

Provision Mapping	Yes	No	Needs developing
Are class Provision Maps drafted by class teachers?			
Do the Provision Maps show the key data including targets and entry and exit data?			
Are targets SMART?			
Can the Provision Map help teachers track pupil absence from the classroom?			
Are class Provision Maps evaluated by class teachers?			
Are evaluated Provision Maps used to support applications for external support or statutory assessment?			
Are intervention target sheets used to record key data for each intervention and a simple system for sharing information between TA and teacher?			
Are interventions prioritised and is the number of interventions proposed reducing over time?			

Table 8.6 Sharing information

Sharing information	Yes	No	Needs developing
Do teachers share anonymised versions of the Provision Map with all parents at parent consultation meetings?			
Do parents understand the interventions in place for their child and how they can support their child?			
Are Provision Maps shared with support staff, temporary staff, volunteers, etc.?			
Are evaluated Provision Maps used to calculate the impact of interventions across the school?			
Is this shared with governors and incorporated into the school's self-evaluation in an easy-to-read format?			
Are Provision Maps used to support requests for support or statutory assessment?			
Are pupil views collected and acted upon?			
Even though we share the Provision Map, do we maintain confidentiality?			

Table 8.7 Training and development

Development	Yes	No	Needs developing
Do we triangulate information from pupil progress data analysis, observation and work scrutiny to determine any areas for development?			
Do we have timetabled opportunities for staff to share good practice and update their Provision Map three times per year?			
Are we using the IDP materials to enhance staff understanding of effective ways of meeting the most commonly occurring is educational needs?			
Do we observe the delivery of interventions and through this identify any training and development needs among support staff?			
Are our support staff members being set appropriate pupil progress targets as part of their performance management?			
Do we have a performance management cycle that is linked to the pupil progress review cycle and thus able to influence the setting and review of targets?			
Do we get good value for money from training? Does our school evaluate and disseminate training to other staff, enter it into the school's self-evaluation and share that evaluation with governors?			

The outcome of this self-review should help you to generate an action plan and direct you to where most work needs to be done to ensure that the introduction of this system is successful. This will enable you to respond to a number of critical questions. For instance:

*   Do your assessment methods need changing?
*   Do you need to improve moderation?
*   Do you need to overhaul pupil progress review meetings to make them more effective?

For most schools, the introduction of the concept of Provision Mapping to teachers and their responsibility for pupils accessing interventions is often the most problematic. In order to support you with this I have provided a PowerPoint presentation that may be used in a twilight staff meeting session with your teachers and support staff. It should take approximately one and a half to two hours to deliver and is designed to prompt discussion. I would recommend that the presentation is delivered by a member of the SLT, preferably the headteacher and not the SENCO, so that staff members understand that Provision Mapping applies to all pupils, not just those with SEN.

To access the PowerPoint presentation, as well as other eResources for this title, please go to www.routledge.com/9780415530309

Although not a system for SENCOs, the SENCO will have a key role to play in ensuring that the school has a clear picture of the impact of interventions over time. The calendar shown in Table 8.8 has been constructed to show the involvement a SENCO should have in the various aspects of the system throughout the year and should be adapted for schools that will assess and review less frequently than six times per year.

SENCOs should see some reduction in workload as management of IEPs and communication with parents should both be reduced. Parents will become better informed by class teachers at parent consultation meetings about the progress their child is making and the intervention in place to help accelerate it where necessary, and should have less need to meet with the SENCO to discuss progress or intervention. Preparation for statutory assessment should be aided by the constant review of what has worked for a pupil and the evaluative Provision Maps can provide valuable evidence with no need for alteration save for anonymisation.

Just as there is nothing new in this system, there is nothing – no initiatives, no programmes or strategies – that will go out of date. Irrespective of national or local policy, schools will always need to know how well their pupils are doing, what needs to be done to help them make better progress and whether it has worked. Schools will always need to share information with governing bodies, parents and outside agencies, and schools will always need to self-evaluate and plan for further development. Despite all the challenges schools face in trying to navigate their way through the endless series of complex policy changes it is vital that they maintain their core values: remembering that children are all different and that our job as teachers is to make sure that they all enjoy and engage in school life in its broadest sense as well as making good progress. Whether your school is an academy or a maintained school this system should be central to all that you do to improve outcomes for pupils, and right at the very heart of it sits the Provision Map, a tool for collecting and collating all the information.

Table 8.8 SENCO annual calendar

SENCO calendar	Term 1	Term 2	Term 3	Term 4	Term 5	Term 6
Week 1	Support baseline assessment	Parent consultation	Moderation P scales	Parent consultation		
Week 2	Audit support staff skills	Performance management Target-setting Support staff	Lead professional development meeting	Performance management review meeting Support staff		
Week 3	Lead professional development meeting	Moderation Speaking and listening	Observations of speech and language/ C&I intervention	Evaluate parent and pupil questionnaires for impact of provision Report to governors	Moderation maths	Lead professional development meeting
Week 4	Moderation reading	Report to governors on evaluation of interventions	Moderation writing		Observation maths intervention	Performance management review meeting Support staff
Week 5	Observation of reading intervention		Analyse data	Analyse data		Analyse data
Week 6			Collate and evaluate provision	Collate and evaluate provision	Analyse data	Support transition Collate and evaluate provision Report to parents Report to governors
Week 7	Analyse data	Analyse Data			Collate and evaluate provision	
Week 8	Collate and evaluate provision	Collate and evaluate provision				

If you embed this system of evaluative Provision Mapping into your school you will be able to answer affirmatively all the questions posed at the start of this book:

- You will have systems for tracking pupil progress embedded in your school.
- You will know what progress is being made by individuals and by groups in your school.
- You will be doing something about progress that is stalled or inadequate.
- All class teachers will have full responsibility and accountability for all pupils in their class, including those with SEN.
- You will be able to tell what the impact is of your additional interventions.
- You will know whether you are getting value for money.
- Your governors will be sufficiently well informed to be able to make suitable challenges.
- Parents will be confident that your school is doing all it can to meet their child's needs.

I believe that our duty as educators requires us to ensure that all children are enjoying, participating and achieving in schools. I also believe that we have a duty to ensure that teachers are enabled to maintain an accurate view of the attainment and achievement of all pupils in their class with a minimum of bureaucracy; that they can easily identify children who need additional intervention without recourse to labelling them SEN and that those children make accelerated progress. I believe that parents want and need better, contextualised information about the provision available and should be better able to understand how to help their child at home. I have seen how the approaches I have set out in this book have helped many schools to ensure that this is happening. I hope that your school is able to use this book to achieve similar outcomes.

Bibliography

Ainscow, M. (ed.) (1991) *Effective Schools for All*. London: Fulton.

Ainscow, M. (1999) *Understanding the Development of Inclusive Schools*. Oxon: Routledge Falmer.

Ainscow, M. (2005a) 'From special education to effective schools for all'. Keynote presentation at the International Special Education Conference, Glasgow, Scotland.

Ainscow, M. (2005) 'Developing inclusive education systems: what are the levers for change?' *Journal of Educational Change* 6(2).

Ainscow, M. and Farrell, P. (2003). *Using Research to Encourage the Development of Inclusive Practices. Making Special Education Inclusive*. London: Fulton.

Ainscow, M. and Miles, S. (2008) 'Making Education for All inclusive: Where next?' University of Manchester, UK Paper prepared for *Prospects*, February.

Ainscow, M., Booth, T., Dyson, A. with Farrell, P., Frankham, J., Gallanaugh, F., Howes, A. and Smith, R. (2006) *Improving Schools, Developing Inclusion*. Oxon: Routledge.

Allen, J. (2003) 'Productive pedagogies and the challenge of inclusion'. *British Journal of Special Education* 30(4): 175–179.

Altrichter, H., Feldman, A., Posch, P. and Somekh, B. (2000) *Teachers Investigate Their Work*. London and New York: Routledge.

Assessment Reform Group (1999) *Assessment for Learning: Beyond the Black Box*. Cambridge: University of Cambridge School of Education.

Bamburg, J. (1994) Excerpted from the NCREL monograph, *Raising Expectations to Improve Student Learning*. NCREL.

Beckhard, R. (1969) *Organization Development: Strategies and Models*. Reading, MA: Addison-Wesley.

Black, P., Gardner, J. and Wiliam, D. (2008) Joint Memorandum on Reliability of Assessments. Submitted to the Children, Schools and Families Committee. In *Testing and Assessment. Third Report of Session 2007–2008*. Norwich: The Stationery Office.

Black Hawkins, K., Florian, L. and Rouse, M. (2007) *Achievement and Inclusion in Schools*. London and New York: Routledge.

Blatchford, P., Bassett, P., Brown, P., Martin, C., Russell, A. and Webster, R. (2009) *Deployment and Impact of Support Staff Project*. London: Institute of Education, University of London.

Booth, T. (1999) *From Special Needs Education to Education for all, a Discussion Document*. Paris: UNESCO.

Booth, T. and Ainscow, M. (eds) (1998) *From Them to Us: An International Study of Inclusion in Education*. London: Routledge.

Booth, T. and Ainscow, M. (revised 2002) *Index for Inclusion*. CSIE.

Corbett, J. (2001) *Supporting Inclusive Education: A Connective Pedagogy*. Oxon: Routledge Falmer.

Costa, A.L. and Kallick, B. (1993) 'Through the lens of a critical friend'. *Educational Leadership* 51(2): 50.

DCSF (2004) *Intensifying Support Programme*. London: Stationery Office.

DCSF (2007) *Primary National Strategy: Pupil Progress Meetings, Prompts and Guidance.* London: Stationery Office.

DCSF (2009a) *Progression Guidance.* DCSF ref: 00553-2009BKT-EN.

DCSF (2009b) *Deployment and Impact of Support Staff in Schools.* DCSF-RR148/DCSF-RB148.

DfES (2003) *Raising Standards and Tackling Workload: A National Agreement.* DfES ref: 0172 2003.

DfES (2004a) *Removing Barriers to Achievement.* DfES ref: 0117/2004D35/PPSTERL/0804/83.

DfES (2004b) *Every Child Matters.* DfES ref: 0786/2004.

DfES (2006) *Effective Leadership: Ensuring the Progress of Pupils with SEN and/or Disabilities.* London: Stationery Office.

DfES (2007) *Making Great Progress: Schools with Outstanding Rates of Progression in Key Stage 2.* DfES ref: 00443-2007BKT-EN.

DfES/DCSF (2009) *The Improving Schools Programme Handbook*, DCSF ref: 00314-2009BKT-EN.

DfE (2010) *The Importance of Teaching.* The Schools White Paper 2010 ref: CM 7980.

DfE (2011a) *Achievement for All National Evaluation.* Final Report. DFE Ref: RR176, November.

DfE (2011b) *Support and Aspiration: A New Approach to Special Educational Needs and Disability: A Consultation.* Norwich: TSO.

DfE (2011c) *Teachers' Standards in England from 2012.* DfE ref: V1.0 0711.

Delamont, S. (2002) *Fieldwork in Educational Settings: Methods, Pitfalls and Perspectives.* London and New York: Routledge.

Durrant, J. and Holden, G. (2006) *Teachers Leading Change: Doing Research for School Improvement.* London: Paul Chapman.

Ekins, A. and Grimes, P. (2009) *Inclusion: Developing an Effective Whole School Approach.* New York: McGraw-Hill.

Frederickson, N. and Cline, T. (2006) *Special Educational Needs, Inclusion and Diversity, A Textbook.* Milton Keynes: Open University Press.

Fullan, M. (ed.) (1993) *The Challenge of School Change: A Collection of Articles.* Arlington, IL: IRI/SkyLight Training and Publishing.

Fullan, M. (2003) *Change Forces with a Vengeance.* London: Routledge Falmer.

Gronn, P. (2003) *The New Work of Educational Leaders: Changing Leadership Practice in an Era of School Reform.* London: Sage.

Gross, J. (2008) *Beating Bureaucracy in Special Educational Needs.* London and New York: Routledge and NASEN.

Gross, J. and White, A. (2003) *Special Educational Needs and School Improvement.* London: Fulton.

Hanko, G. (1999) *Increasing Competence through Collaborative Problem Solving.* Oxon: Fulton.

Hart, S. (1996) *Beyond Special Needs: Enhancing Children's Learning Through Innovative Thinking.* London: Paul Chapman.

Hart, S., Dixon, A., Drummond, M.J. and McIntyre, with Brach, N., Conway, C., Madigan, N., Marchall, J., Peacock, A., Reay, A., Tahibet, Y., Worrall, N. and Yarker, P. (2004) *Learning without Limits.* Milton Keynes: Open University Press, McGraw-Hill Education.

Higgins, S., Kokotsaki, D. and Coe, R. (2011) *Toolkit of Strategies to Improve Learning: Summary for Schools Spending the Pupil Premium.* Sutton Trust, Centre for Evaluation and Monitoring, May.

Hopkins, D. (2007) *Every School a Great School.* Milton Keynes: Open University Press, McGraw-Hill Education.

Howes, A., Davies, S.M.B. and Fox, S. (2009) *Improving the Context for Inclusion: Personalising Teacher Development through Collaborative Action Research.* London and New York: Routledge.

Kuglemass, J.W. (2004) *The Inclusive School: Sustaining Equity and Standards.* New York: Teachers College Press.

Lamb, B. (2009) *SEN and Parental Confidence.* London: Crown Copyright.

MacBeath, J. (2009) 'Border crossings'. *Improving Schools* 12: 81–92.

MacBeath, J. (2007) 'School inspection and self-evaluation: working with the new relationship'. *Improving Schools* 10(199). University of Edinburgh, Routledge.

Meadmore, D. (2001) 'The pursuit of standards: simply managing education?' *International Journal of Inclusive Education* 5(4): 353–365, available online at: <http://ejournals.ebsco.com/direct.asp?ArticleID=8G35PHMEKEHF2TWATULX> (accessed 20 August 2009).

Mitchell, D. (2008) *What Really Works in Special and Inclusive Education: Using Evidence-based Teaching Strategies*. London and New York: Routledge.

Ofsted (2004a) *A New Relationship with Schools*. Office for Standards in Education.

Ofsted (2004b) *Special Educational Needs and Disability, Towards Inclusive Schools*. Office for Standards in Education.

Ofsted (2010a) *Special Educational Needs and/or Disabilities in Mainstream Schools: A Briefing Paper for section 5 Inspectors*. Office for Standards in Education.

Ofsted (2010b) *Workforce Reform in Schools: Has it Made a Difference?* Office for Standards in Education.

Ofsted (2010c) *Special Educational Needs and Disability Review: A Statement is not Enough*. Office for Standards in Education, ref: 090221.

Ofsted (2011) *Subsidiary Guidance: Supporting the Inspection of Maintained Schools and Academies from January 2012*. Office for Standards in Education, ref: 110166.

Ofsted (2012) *The Evaluation Schedule for the Inspection of Maintained Schools and Academies from January 2012*. Office for Standards in Education, ref: 090098.

Qualifications and Curriculum Authority (2009) *Research into Marking Quality: Studies to Inform Future Work on National Curriculum Assessment*. London: QCA.

Randall, M. and Thornton, B. (2001) *Advising and Supporting Teachers*. Cambridge: Cambridge University Press.

Robson, C. (2002) *Real World Research* (2nd edn). Oxford: Blackwell.

Rouse, M. and Florian, L. (2006) 'Inclusion and achievement: student achievement in secondary schools with higher and lower proportions of pupils designated as having special educational needs'. *International Journal of Inclusive Education* 10(6): 481–494.

The Lancet (2011) Article. *The Lancet* 378(9801): 1485–1492.

UNESCO (1994) *The Salamanca Statement and Framework for Action on Special Needs Education*. Madrid: UNESCO.

UNICEF (2007) 'Child poverty in perspective: an overview of child well-being in rich countries.' *Innocenti Report Card* 7, UNICEF Innocenti Research Centre, Florence.

West, M., Ainscow, M. and Stanford, J. (2005)'Sustaining improvement in schools in challenging circumstances: a study of successful practice'. *School Leadership & Management* 25(1):77–93.

Whitehead, J. and McNiff, J. (2006) *Action Research Living Theory*. London: Sage.

Wrigley, T. (2006) *Another School is Possible*. London: Bookmarks Publications and Trentham Books.

Index

Note: Page numbers followed by 't' refer to tables.